OLD ENOUGH TO KNOW

What Teenagers Need to Know
About Life and Relationships

Michael W. Smith

& Fritz Ridenour

Tommy
NELSON

Thomas Nelson, Inc.
Nashville

Published in Nashville, Tennessee, by Tommy Nelson™, a division of Thomas Nelson, Inc.

Scripture references are from the following sources:

The Holy Bible, New International Version (NIV). Copyright © 1973, 1978, 1984 International Bible Society. Used by permission of Zondervan Bible Publishers.

The Holy Bible, New Living Translation (NLT). Copyright © 1996. Used by permission of Tyndale House Publishers, Inc., Wheaton, Illinois.

The Living Bible (TLB). Copyright © 1971 by Tyndale House Publishers, Wheaton, Illinois. Used by permission.

The New King James Version (NKJV). Copyright © 1979, 1980, 1982, Thomas Nelson, Inc., Publisher. All rights reserved.

Library of Congress Cataloging-in-Publication Data

Smith, Michael W. (Michael Whitaker)
   Old enough to know.

   Summary: Discusses critical adolescent issues such as drugs, sexuality, peer pressure, and independence, with some autobiographical material from the author's life and letters he has received.

   1. Teenagers—Religious life. 2. Smith, Michael W. (Michael Whitaker)—Juvenile literature [1. Adolescence. 2. Conduct of life. 3. Christian life. 4. Smith, Michael W. (Michael Whitaker)]
   1. Ridenour, Fritz. II. Title.
BV4531.2.S59 1988 248.8'3 89-5276
ISBN 0-8499-7604-9 (previously 0-8499-3162-2, 0-8344-0153-3)

Printed in the U.S.A.

00 01 02 03 04 05 PHX 9 8 7 6 5 4 3 2 1

Dedicated to my mom and dad,
who not only brought me into this life
but have taught me how to end it
in His glory.

Introduction:
This Book Is for My Friends

I've never written a book before. It's kind of weird—trying to put down on paper why I write my songs. It's a lot easier to sit down at a piano and just tinker with a tune that keeps flirting with my mind, and finally work it out. Writing books is a *lot* harder.

It reminds me of a question a reporter for a Christian TV station asked one night in the dressing room before a concert. With his mini-cam rolling, he said, "Tell me, Michael, what's God been doing in your life?"

At first, I wasn't sure how to answer. What did this guy want? A full rundown? Was he checking me out? I decided to do what I've always done—be up front and just say it: "He's doing all kinds of things. We're out here on this tour with a high-energy rock-'n'-roll show, and our number one priority is to encourage kids and let them know God thinks they're OK."

These days I find a lot of kids—not to mention quite a few adults—who really don't believe they're OK. And the pressure's coming from every direction to try all kinds of things. I get letters every week from kids who are struggling with heavy questions and problems. I've always tried to read as many letters as I can and answer them personally, if possible. Then I had an idea: Why not do an entire album that talks about these problems? And so we did *The Big Picture* to let kids know we hear them and care.

For this book I've taken lyrics from twelve of my songs, most of them right off *The Big Picture* album. I want to tell you what's behind these lyrics and to share parts of my life that might help you realize that "I've been there," and I know how it feels.

Another reason I'm writing this book is that I believe you're old enough to know the difference between the phony and the genuine, that you won't be fooled into confusing real love with what some very mixed-up people say love should be.

One of the most important parts of this book will be excerpts from letters written by teenagers and young adults telling me what's happening in their lives. Their letters say it better than I ever could, and I know they won't mind my sharing them with as many people as possible. Where necessary, I've changed names, places, and ages to protect privacy. But I can tell you that every letter I quote is from someone who lives where you live—in the real world where life is tough and friends are very hard to find.

This book is my letter to you as I share what is important to me. I am not a psychologist, and I don't suggest that I have all the answers to life. I am simply telling my struggles and my victories. If you have serious problems, I urge you to seek professional help. Some excellent sources of help are listed in the back of this book.

I really mean it when I say this book is for my friends—friends I've already made and friends I don't know yet but want very much to meet. My best friend on this planet, my wife, Debbie, wrote the words to a song called "Friends," and everywhere we play, the kids sing it with us.

"Friends" is the high point of every concert for me because we are really singing about Someone who is the Ultimate Friend. He's the One who made it all. He's the real reason we're out there pounding the highways, playing in gyms, hockey rinks, and auditoriums—everywhere we can—to let people know He's their friend. He's the real reason you and I can be friends and stay friends. Friends are friends forever when the Lord's the Lord of them!

Contents

1

Can You Believe You're Worth It?

Kids ask me all the time, in one way or another, "Can God really think much of me? Nobody else does!" For example, I got a letter from Jill, who said, "I'm really going through some tough times now. I guess the main reason is my real lack of self-esteem. I don't like myself and neither does anyone else, it seems."

I can't help but think we did the song "You're Alright" for someone just like Jill. As the first verse says:

> You take a look inside . . . but you don't like what you see . . . And so you choose to look away . . . It doesn't coincide . . . with how you'd like to be . . . And each glimpse of hope can easily fade.

According to Jill's letter, lots of things are going wrong. Some are no big deal, but they still hurt. Her older sister gets straight A's and all the praise and encouragement. Jill is lucky to pull C's and a few D's. But she says a far bigger problem is this:

> I'm bulimic and I've tried and tried and tried to lose this weight but I can't. And I've talked to God about it, and He wants me to lose it and get my self-esteem back. I know He does. But I'm hitting such a depression. What's wrong with me? What am I going to do after I graduate? When am I going to lose this weight? When am I going to have such a wonderful, peaceful energetic life with Christ?

Jill Needs More than Easy Answers

You know, it's real easy to think, *I've got all the answers* for people with problems. Why, all I have to do is quote the chorus of "You're Alright" for Jill. That should take care of everything, shouldn't it?

Down on your confidence . . . it's a fight that won't let go . . . But you've got to realize that you're alright . . . 'Cause under your rubble . . . lies a heart the Father holds . . . And when you see your life through His eyes . . . you're alright.

But as Jill's letter goes on to say: "'You're Alright' is really a great song and I want to believe it, but I can't. I get *so* lonely and I tell God my fears, my dislikes, the things I love . . . I want to have a great relationship with God and be loving and caring naturally, not just a put-on."

Have you ever felt like Jill? I have. I know what it's like to want to believe something but not to be able to put it together. I grew up in a "good Christian home" and went to church most of my life, but then in late high school and during a couple of years of college I thought I had to "try a few things." Music had always been my thing, and I left home at twenty to "make it big" as a musician. But all I seemed to make it into was a lot of confusion and trouble.

Just What Is Self-Esteem?

When Jill talks about losing her self-esteem, I understand. There are all kinds of definitions for self-esteem or self-image.

I like the one that explains it as "the deep-down feeling you have about what you are worth." In other words, it's simply your own opinion of yourself and your personal value. It boils down to saying, "I like myself," or "I can't stand myself!"

One way to look at your self-esteem is to compare it to a three-legged stool. The three "legs" that hold up your self-esteem are all statements that begin with "I am":

1. *I am accepted.* I feel loved, wanted, and needed.
2. *I am important.* I feel worthwhile and valuable—to myself as well as others.
3. *I am capable.* I can handle things. I can do it![1]

Two major influences that work to build up or tear down anyone's self-esteem are parents and peer group. A lot of high school kids and college-age people write to me, longing for family or friends who could just give them an even break. Instead, their parents are destroying their self-esteem with accusations like "You don't try hard enough" or "You're a slob" or "You're worthless."

When things at home are tense, it's bad enough, but when they are bad at school, too, it can be murder. Pete wrote to tell me he gets up every morning to go to school, but he hates it. His letter said: "I've got no real friends there. I get teased, tormented, and pushed around. It's a living hell . . . I got no ambition left . . . All I want is a friend, but is there such a thing? . . . I pray and talk to the Lord and try to convince myself I'm an all right person, but I'm sick of playing that game."

God Has Good News for You

The good news for Pete is that he doesn't have to convince God he's all right because God already thinks so! God does not play games with anyone's self-esteem. He gave us our self-esteem in the first place. No matter how tough things may get at home or at school, or anywhere else, you can hang on to this:

> God just plain likes you, no matter who you are, where you are, or what kind of mess you may think you are or think that you're in.

How can I be so sure of that? I just go to Psalm 139, my favorite part of the Bible. One thing that makes this psalm so meaningful to me is that it is written by a musician—David, the psalmist, player of the harp, and singer of songs for King Saul. In Psalm 139 he wrote about how well God knows us: "O LORD, you have searched me and you know me. You know when I sit and when I rise; you perceive my thoughts from afar. You discern my going out and my lying down; you are familiar with all my ways" (Ps. 139:1–3, NIV).

A little farther on, David talks about how God made each of us:

> For you created my inmost being; you knit me together in my mother's womb. I praise you because I am fearfully and wonderfully made; your works are wonderful, I know that full well. My frame was not hidden from you when I was made in the secret place. When I was woven together in the depths of the earth, your eyes saw

my unformed body. All the days ordained for me
were written in your book before one of them
came to be. (Ps. 139:13–16, NIV)

I believe we are all born to have good self-esteem because
we are made by God, in His image. And, as some bumper
sticker philosopher said, "God don't make no junk." Why is it,
then, that we sometimes feel like junk? Is it God's fault? Is it
the architect's fault if the building gets dirty and run down?
No, we mess ourselves up.

Jill has messed herself up with too much weight. She
knows it, and she tries and tries to lose it, but she hasn't had
any luck—yet.

Actually, Jill isn't looking for luck; she's looking for the
power to finally conquer her weight problem, and she can
have it, just as you can have the power you need to conquer
your problem, whatever it is.

Trusting God Does Work!

I know trusting God works because I finally messed up bad
enough to realize I couldn't do it on my own. Sometimes it
sounds a little offhand when someone talks about "not being
able to do it on my own and so I just trusted God." It can
seem just a little too easy. I've got a hunch that's a problem for
a lot of us—if it's too simple, we don't think it will work.

I found out that trusting God is easier said than done. But
please believe me, it *does work*. And in trusting Him you find
something very important. You find out He really does love
you—warts, extra weight, and all. There's another verse of
Scripture I like in one of Paul's letters where he says: "When

we were utterly helpless with no way of escape, Christ came at just the right time and died for us sinners who had no use for him. Even if we were good, we really wouldn't expect anyone to die for us, though, of course, that might be barely possible. But God showed his great love for us by sending Christ to die for us while we were yet sinners" (Rom. 5:6–8, TLB).

I believe that God's love—a love so great that He was willing to die for us—is the best reason of all to have good self-esteem, no matter how bad things are. In another letter, Paul tells us that Christ is the One who made it all (Col. 1:15–17). Christ is actually the Creator Lord that David is talking to in Psalm 139. That means that when Christ died for you and me, He knew all about us even though we weren't born yet!

Christ knew the total life story of every one of us. He knew if we'd be smart or just average. He knew if we'd be athletic, good-looking, thin, or overweight. He knew if we'd be part of the woodwork or popular. In her letter, Jill had some angry thoughts about popularity:

> One of the words I detest more than anything else is "popular." If you're not "popular" no one likes you at church. If you're not "popular" the younger kids don't treat you with awe or respect like the cheerleaders. What right do people have to do this? Them having the time of their life and I can't wait to get out of there.

What can I say to Jill? What can I say to so many kids who don't think they're popular or attractive or smart or thin enough or heavy enough or fast enough or strong enough? It all boils down to "I don't think I'm good enough!"

I believed the same thing for a while, but I was fortunate enough to realize it was a lie Satan was using to destroy my life. I know how it feels to wrestle against evil spiritual forces, and I'll tell you more about it in chapters two and three.

You Can Shut Satan Down

I am totally convinced there is nothing Satan would like better than to destroy everyone he can. Unfortunately, he's having a lot of success with too many people, but there is a way to turn him off and shut him down. It's all tied in with really understanding that God does love you—*unconditionally.*

As the final verse of "You're Alright" puts it:

```
To learn how He loves you . . . is to learn
to love yourself . . . to live the life He's liv-
ing in you . . . And what others think of you
. . . could never measure to the wealth . . . of
what He's paid and given to you.
```

No question about it, the most important song we do in any concert is "You're Alright." When Christ walked among us down here on earth, He kept telling people, "You're all right, . . . if you have faith in Me."

He told people, "You're all right," and their paralysis vanished, and they walked and jumped and danced for joy.

He told people, "You're all right," and they could see and hear again.

He told one woman, "You're all right" when some self-righteous hypocrites were ready to stone her to death. And then He forgave her and told her to go and sin no more.

When He went to the cross, He told the whole world, "Believe in Me. Believe in what I am doing for you, and you will be all right. This is the highest price I can pay, and I pay it with no strings attached. Go and sin no more."

Remember—under the rubble of your problems and your worries lies a heart the Father holds, and if you can see your life the way He sees it—paid for by His own Son—then you'll know you're all right!

2

Are You Who You Say You Are?

H ave you ever thought about how it would feel to be a double agent? Think of all the sweaty-palmed times you'd have, reporting first to one side and then to the other in some big, international spy/counterspy duel.

Being a double agent sounds like fun. You can play both sides against each other and try to collect at both ends. It looks exciting in the movies. In real life, though, it's the pits.

I started living as a double agent during my senior year in high school. I became a hypocrite who played both ends against the middle, but all I collected was a big bag of guilties.

By day I was good ol' Smitty, pillar of righteousness, faithful attender of church and Bible study. The older ladies would come by and give me a peck on the cheek and tell me how wonderful I was. I loved being involved at church. I *wanted* to be there, but unfortunately I wanted to be some other places, too.

The "Flood Wall"

By night I was one of the guys at the "Flood Wall," one of the favorite spots to "hang out" in our little town of Kenova, West Virginia. Kenova is a little town of about four thousand, which perches on the banks of the mighty Ohio River, right where West Virginia, Ohio, and Kentucky meet. (That's how Kenova got its name—KEN for Kentucky, O for Ohio, and VA for West Virginia.)

Every spring in Kenova we need that Flood Wall to hold back the mighty Ohio if it decides to go a little crazy. The Wall is three miles long, higher than a two-story house, sloping on both sides and a great place to do a lot of things. In the fall, our football team ran up and down the Wall to get in shape; in the winter it was great for sleds and toboggans; in the spring the top of the Wall was a perfect spot for flying kites. And all year around, the Flood Wall was the place for smoking pot and drinking beer "after hours."

It was at the Flood Wall that I finally got talked into having my first joint. Did I enjoy it? Did I get high? All I can remember is that I felt guilty and very depressed because I certainly knew better. I'd been brought up in a Christian family and started going to church before I could even remember. All my life, especially through junior high and the first part of high school, I'd been walking the line with the Lord, saying "no" to all the invitations to drink and do drugs.

Back in eighth grade I had become part of a group that got together regularly for what you could call "mega Bible studies." We really dug into books like Paul's letters to the Romans. There I was, just a little squirt with a bunch of older guys. I got into it—I really did. I used to wear this big cross and carry a thick Bible. To some extent I guess I was a "Jesus freak," but I didn't care. I was sold on Christ—it was all very real to me.

I Was "Super Christian" Until . . .

I went along like that through most of my junior year, wearing my cross, lugging my Bible everywhere, attending rallies and Fellowship of Christian Athlete meetings and going to Bible studies twice a week.

By the time I was a junior, life was very full. I had joined the high school youth chorus, where I could play the piano and sing. And I tried out for the football team and made the squad as a kicker and substitute offensive end. Football was *the* sport at C-K High. Its teams still go to the state finals almost every year.

Joining the football team was good—and bad—for me. The good part came from being coached by men like Carl Ward and his assistant Dale Craycraft. Both of them attended our church, and Dale taught a Sunday school class that I attended throughout my high school years.

But the bad part of playing with the football team was that I started hanging out with some people who weren't good for me at all. When they wanted to head for the Flood Wall, I went along because I wanted to be part of them. But maybe I needed something else even more. I think I needed to find out "what I had been missing." I've always been a little daring and willing to take a risk. I thought I could fool around with The System and get away with it. How wrong I was.

By the time I was a senior I was really "Goin' Thru the Motions." A lot of kids tell me they know exactly what the first verse of that song is trying to say:

Actions have been justified . . . all is compromised . . . looking for approval there . . . in someone else's eyes . . . Dodging all you really are . . . becomes your greatest task . . . acting out your lonely part . . . you hide behind your mask.

The worst thing about wearing a mask is that you can't be yourself—and that's a lonely way to live. But I tried it anyway. There were nights when I literally went from church meetings to the Flood Wall to drink beer or occasionally smoke pot with my so-called friends. I really didn't do that much of either one, but I wanted to fit in. After all, when two starting linebackers offer you a beer, it's pretty hard to say no.

I Was Reckless, but God Was Loving

When I did my Flood Wall thing, did I think I was Mr. Big? That I was getting away with something? Putting one over on the church establishment? Showing them I could do as I pleased? No! My bag of guilties just got bigger. As "Goin' Thru the Motions" goes on to say:

Never true to yourself . . . knowing well this is not like you . . . Fooling yourself . . . you're just living a lie.

I really can't explain it, and I'm not proud of it. I'm just being honest, to let you know I can identify with anyone who's struggling with trying to live the right way and not making it.

Whatever you think, don't take my confessions and say, "See, Michael W. Smith went out and lived a little and it didn't hurt him. Today he's doing just great!" Forget that kind of talk because it's simply not true. I still carry emotional and spiritual scars that I believe God allowed to bring me back to Him. The truth is, I was stupid and reckless—and lucky, if a Christian can be lucky. Christian "luck" is really God protecting you and helping you out of the messes you make for yourself.

I'm sharing my mistakes to tell you I know how it feels when life just isn't working. You start asking: What's wrong? Don't I have enough faith? Am I a phony? Am I even really a Christian? Or is it all a bad joke? Who am I *really*?

I've asked myself all those questions and a lot more besides. I found a few of the answers, and I'm still working on others, just as you are. The one thing that really helps is to remember that we're in pretty good company. The guy who wrote over half the New Testament felt the same way!

A Dog Fight Inside

You may know Paul's story. He grew up as part of the Jewish establishment and became a "super Pharisee." They called him Saul back then, and he was so "righteous" he squeaked. But when he met Jesus Christ, he became Paul, the apostle who almost single-handedly spread Christianity throughout the known civilized world. It sounds as if Paul had everything going for him, but not quite. He wrote to Christian friends in the church at Rome and said:

> I don't understand myself at all, for I really want to do what is right, but I can't. I do what I don't want to—what I hate. I know perfectly well that what I am doing is wrong . . . It is sin inside me that is stronger than I am that makes me do these evil things. I know I am rotten through and through so far as my old sinful nature is concerned. No matter which way I turn I can't make myself do right. I want to but I can't . . . sin still has me in its evil grasp. (Romans 7:15–18, 20, TLB)

Paul wrote a lot of great things, but he never wrote anything more important than this. If you can get a handle on what he is saying here, it will tell you who you are—really. It will tell you why becoming a Christian does not mean you will never have another zit, another detention, another ticket or another put-down from somebody you thought was your friend.

There are thousands of kids (and adults) who can't understand why things keep slipping, sliding, and crashing when they try to "walk with the Lord." Well, Paul gives you the straight answer. You still have the old sinful self inside, and it's literally at war with the new person you became in Christ.

It's sort of like the guy who was getting started in a guard dog business. He only had two dogs—a Doberman pinscher and a German shepherd. "Which one is toughest?" somebody asked him. "Who would win in a fight?"

"The one I feed the most," said the owner.

Spiritually speaking, it's like we have two dogs living inside, and we all go through times when one dog gets fed more than the other. That's why Paul admits when he wants to do what is right, it seems he always fails and does what is wrong. This isn't what he really wants. Paul's new, higher nature wants to do God's will, but, for some reason he can't explain, his old, lower nature keeps winning the fight (see Rom. 7:21–23).

What a mess! Does it get any worse than this? Does it even do any good to become a Christian? What's the use? If the lower side of me is in control, am I doomed? I get letters that ask all these questions and more.

How Far Is Too Far?

Kari wrote to tell me her friends have been pushing her to drink, do drugs, and have sex (and not necessarily in that order). Kari keeps saying no, but she wonders:

How far can I go before it's a sin? How much can I fool around with a guy before I'm condemned? How much can I drink before I need to be forgiven? If I can't do any of these things in order to stay straight with God, then I won't do any. But I'm so lonely. All my friends live "sinful" lives and seem none the worse. I feel so different and weird and so alone because I won't do these things anymore. . . . But I'm not happy not doing these things either. Why can't I find happiness on either side? What's wrong with me??!!

I don't have any easy answers to give Kari about feeling lonely and unhappy. That one always comes down to what kind of friends are worth having. If you can't find friends with the same values and beliefs you have, you are in for a tough time.

What about people who live like the devil and don't seem to have as many problems as you do? The answer to that one is pretty plain. If you have nothing going with Jesus, Satan has you in his pocket. He'll make it as easy as he can to keep you thinking, *Who needs God?*

But when you decide that you and Jesus will be friends forever, that's when the trouble starts. Then Satan likes nothing better than to make you think you're a flake and a phony. He wants you to think you have to be "real good," sort of like making your quota every week.

Satan loves questions like "How far can I go before it's a sin?" and "How much can I fool around with a guy before I'm condemned?" and "How much can I drink before I need to be forgiven?" He wants you to think being a Christian is all wrapped up in "being good," and if you're not "good enough" you don't make the grade.

So there you are, caught in a big tug-of-war between what's right and what's wrong, and you're the rope. One side of you wants the old friends and the old ways, while the other side is pulling for new life. All of a sudden you're actually caught in the middle of the chorus of "Goin' Thru the Motions":

```
Goin' thru the motions . . . victim of the cir-
cumstance . . . prisoner of the shame . . . But
it's the double standard life . . . That keeps
you in the game . . . Taken by your own disguise
. . . but when it's wearing thin . . . you'll do
anything it takes . . . to impress your friends.
```

It's your choice. You're the only one who can choose. Kari knows it, and that's why she says, "If I can't do any of these things in order to stay straight with God, then I won't do any. But I'm so lonely."

I know the feeling. You feel as if you've dug yourself a deep hole and there's no way out. You can't see anybody up there wanting to throw you a rope, but wait a minute, look again. Somebody is up there with a rope after all! If all Paul had written was "bad news" about being a slave to his old lower self, life would be really bleak. But Paul says there is an answer:

Who will free me from my slavery to this deadly lower nature? Thank God! It has been done by Jesus Christ our Lord. He has set me free. So there is now no condemnation awaiting those who belong to

Christ Jesus. For the power of the life-giving Spirit
. . . has freed me from the vicious circle of sin and
death. (Rom. 7:24–8:2, TLB)

God Doesn't Keep Score

Talk about good news! God isn't sitting up there keeping score on how far you go or how much you drink. As long as you are on Christ's team, it's a whole new ball game. You don't have to worry about batting .500 or even .250. Christ has already hit the home run.

When you've made a commitment to be on Christ's team and you're trying to stay in the game, you don't get condemned for making errors. He took care of all your errors when He died on the cross. So it's never a question of how far you can go before you will be condemned. God will let you go as far as you want to go, but you will start feeling miserable. The Holy Spirit will use your conscience to tell you you're only going through the motions. You'll know you're not being true to who you really are and what you really want to be.

If you give in to pressure to lie, cheat, be selfish, do drugs, drink, or have sex, *of course* you'll feel miserable. Remember Psalm 139? God goes everywhere with you. He knows your every move.

Oh, you can change the game plan, and you can take wrong turns and hang out with wrong people, but God still has His hand on you. When you fool around with the bad stuff, things can get uncomfortable. You'll feel like Kari, not thinking you can find happiness on *either* side. Well, it's plain to see you won't find any happiness on the side with the old crowd and the old ways and the same old routine of drinking, drugs, and sex. If God is real in your life, that stuff has to bother you because it's not part of His program for you.

What's the answer? Well, it certainly isn't suicide or selling out to The System of secular society. Instead, sit down and think it through. You can't be saved by keeping all the laws because nobody can really keep them completely. It's not like playing horseshoes. You don't come close or throw a leaner. You toss a ringer every time or forget it. You can try to keep every law of God, but make one little slip and you're just as guilty as the one who has broken every law there is (see James 2:10).

You Can Win the Battle . . . IF

But God's new game plan doesn't call for perfect performance. His new plan means: You can defeat your old evil nature . . . IF. You can do what your new nature wants you to do . . . IF. You can obey God's laws . . . IF.

What's the big "IF"? Paul tells us in Romans 8:4–5, "We can obey God's laws if we follow after the Holy Spirit and no longer obey the old evil nature within us. Those who let themselves be controlled by their lower natures live only to please themselves, but those who follow after the Holy Spirit find themselves doing those things that please God" (TLB).

Paul makes sense, all right, but just how do you follow after the Holy Spirit and let Him take control? One way *not* to do it is to run around telling yourself, "I've gotta be good. I've gotta think good thoughts and do lots of good deeds." Try that and you'll be sucked back into the same old living-by-the-rules routine, and you'll wind up frustrated and feeling guilty.

The first thing to do is some "serious business" with God

and let Him know that you really want to be led by the Holy Spirit instead of just living the "I wanna" kind of life. I know from personal experience that this is how it has to start. I made my serious turnaround sitting on the floor of my apartment, crying like a baby, tired of "I wanna" and ready to say, "God, You're in charge."

Once you take that first big step in a new direction, the secret to walking in the Spirit is starting each day with a new vow to live by faith. Yes, I know you've heard that one before, too, but it's still true. When you walk in the Spirit, you don't live to please yourself, the crowd, the peer group, or The System. You live to please God.

That's tough, I know. I regret those times back in high school when I wasn't strong enough to do it. With me, it was more a matter of not having sense enough. I thought I could try just about anything and get away with it. I was very wrong.

I was also pretty self-centered. And maybe I was a little afraid to admit my mistakes to God. Oh, I felt guilty all right. My bag of guilties got bigger all the time. But I don't think I really ever sat down and confessed and told God, "I really want to go in the other direction—I want to follow You and nobody else."

Nobody Is in Your Way but You

I guess it comes down to this. If you really want to walk in the Spirit, nobody's standing in your way but you. It's your life, and God lets you make your own decisions. Why doesn't He make your decisions for you? Why does He leave you with the old evil nature in there fighting with the new nature that wants to follow Him?

I really don't know the whole answer, but it has something to do with the fact that He loves us so much He made us free to make our own choices. We can choose to walk with Him, or we can choose to run away.

In the next chapter I'll tell you about how I tried to run away from God. I was feeling sorry for myself, asking God to give me a break. He did better than that. *He broke me* because He had a plan for me that was far better than anything I ever could have dreamed of.

chapter three

You Can't Run Away

Have you ever dreamed of running away from your problems or responsibilities by escaping to a secret, secluded island paradise somewhere—someplace nobody knows about, where you can just kick back, hang out, and escape the pressure?

There is a place like that—and I'm not talking about Maui or Tahiti, which are about as secret and secluded as your local interstate highway. This island is called "Lamu," and it's located just a few miles off the coast of Kenya in the Indian Ocean.

A few years ago Amy Grant visited her good friend Jeannie, who was teaching African teenagers in a rustic Kenyan village. Jeannie mentioned Lamu, a secluded island that very few people knew about, which was just an hour and a half away by boat. Amy and Jeannie decided to spend a few days on Lamu, and it turned out to be the island paradise everyone dreams about. A hideaway for the "rich and famous," Lamu has blue lagoons with crystal-clear water, white sandy beaches, and absolutely perfect weather.

While on Lamu, Amy and Jeannie struck up conversations with different people to learn why they had come to this fabulous spot. One young guy was from a wealthy Italian family who had shipped him to Lamu to "find himself" before settling down to run the family business. But all he was finding was an endless routine of parties, drugs, and boredom.

Another interesting character was a wealthy Englishman in his mid-forties who filled his days with trying to find pleasure and happiness in a playboy lifestyle. Amy doesn't mince words, and she asked him, "What's the point of all this?"

The Englishman gave her a jaded, bored look and said,

"Aren't we all just running? Just filling the emptiness by running away?"

When Amy got back from Lamu, we got together to work on *The Big Picture*. I played one tune I was especially excited about, but it needed lyrics. When she heard it, she lit up and said it was perfect for a song about "Lamu."

"We've got to write a song about this," she said, "about people obsessed with running away to find happiness. They're like onions—peeling off layer after layer until there's nothing left."

Lots of Ways to Lamu

We're all tempted to go find our own "Lamu," maybe to run from reality and responsibility. You can go by way of Fort Lauderdale or Palm Springs, or you can hang out with friends playing video games, or you can just sit in your room with the headset on.

Or maybe you want to get away from parents or that someone who deserted or degraded you. It could be those jerks at school who are making life miserable or that sadistic coach or teacher you wish would take a hike to some other school district.

For whatever reason you want to run, the first verse and chorus of "Lamu" catch that feeling:

Here we are on a boat out on the sea . . . off the coast of Africa . . . Heading for peaceful shores . . . with a cast of strangers . . . to an island hideaway . . . I hear you telling me . . . of the place we soon will be . . . a rebirth from life's demise . . . where the world is still . . . It's ideal . . . Anything you dream is real . . . It's Hotel Paradise . . . and you say it's nice when you run to . . . Lamu—far away . . . Leave the pain far behind you . . . hoping it won't find you in Lamu—far away . . . You say it's there that you can run . . . from the one inside of you.

That last line of the chorus is the one that connects with me. I started running from the One inside of me back in high school. I suppose my first "Lamu" was the Flood Wall—not exactly an island paradise but definitely a place to try to get away from responsibilities and to "experience life."

The funny thing is, I didn't have any really good reasons to run from God or anyone else. I had been extremely fortunate, with great parents and good friends at church and school. Compared to many of the kids we talk with across the country, I had good self-esteem and a great life.

I guess eighth grade was a high point. That's when I was in that Bible study group that was really booming. Nothing was ever really planned. We just showed up at Bill Yeoman's place— sometimes there'd be forty of us, sometimes as many as sixty or seventy, all getting together to share and have fun. The Yeomans had kids of their own and really enjoyed opening their home to us. We'd all just sit around and talk. We'd sing songs and have a great time studying and worshiping God.

I was on cloud ten, and I'll always be grateful to Bill Yeoman and his wife for providing those experiences. They were very real in my life, and they left their stamp on me.

There's no doubt—without those times I'm not sure where I'd be today.

But like a lot of good things, our Bible study group seemed to run its course and then fade away. A lot of the older kids started going away to school, getting married, and taking jobs. When I lost that influence from really strong Christians, I started to drift. I think deep inside I was lonely. I started thinking, *Man, I'm going to graduate in a year and a half or so. Then it will be all over. I'd better get into it while I have time!*

I Hated "Studying" Music

So I got into it with the wrong crowd and the wrong friends. After I got out of high school, I tried a year of college at Marshall University in Huntington, about eight miles north of Kenova. I kept going to church, but I always seemed to end up with the other crowd. Instead of the Flood Wall, I did my hanging out by cutting class to play pinball or pool at the local arcade.

I majored in music at Marshall, but I just couldn't get into it. I had to study music theory, but I wasn't interested in theory. Obviously, being disciplined wasn't one of my greatest strong points. I was interested in playing the real thing. I didn't want to teach music, I wanted to perform it. I always felt that somehow I was supposed to reach the world with my music.

As much as I hated college, I stuck it out for a year because I had promised Mom and Dad I would give it a try. I lived at home during that time, so I was driving up to Huntington for classes and knocking around Ceredo and Kenova with friends like Dan, a guy who could have been one of the greatest artists who ever lived.

Dan was so intelligent it was ridiculous, and he had tremendous gifts as a painter. He had been part of the crowd I knew back at church, but he had drifted farther than I had. He knew the Bible like the back of his hand, but he had a bad drinking problem.

Dan and many of my other friends were very supportive of me and my music. Sometimes I'd play something that I had written and they'd say, "Man, you've got to do something with your music. You're wasting yourself here."

So I started feeling sorry for myself. Here I was, frustrated, stuck in a little town like Kenova when I felt I had the gift to do something really great. I knew if I was going to do anything with my music I had to get to Nashville, about three hundred miles away. To get started in music, you have to go to one of three towns: New York, Los Angeles, or Nashville. Nashville was closest, and I also knew someone there who could help me—Shane Keister, a top session keyboard player.

Was Nashville My Lamu?

So in the spring of 1978, I moved. My parents had mixed emotions when I packed my bags for Nashville. They knew that I had been running with a fast crowd and that I probably wouldn't slow down any when I got to Nashville. At the same time, my parents really trusted the Lord and believed I was doing exactly what I was supposed to do.

So I left for Nashville to "make it big in music." Was Nashville my "Lamu"? Not really—not any more than Kenova was at that time of my life. I thought I was running toward a great career in Nashville. Now I realize it didn't matter what town I was living in—I was still running from the One inside of me to do *my* thing, *my* way.

Obviously you can't get away from Someone when you're

carrying Him around inside. God knew exactly what was ahead for me. There are some lines in Psalm 139 that say it all:

> Before a word is on my tongue you know it com-
> pletely, O LORD. You hem me in—behind and
> before; you have laid your hand upon me. Such
> knowledge is too wonderful for me, too lofty for
> me to attain. (Ps. 139:4–6, NIV)

David, the psalmist, realized that God knew him so well it didn't matter where he was. He could be wrestling bears who were after his sheep, firing a stone right between Goliath's eyes, or leading his soldiers in battle. David knew that God knew his every thought, his every move. God is familiar with *all* our ways. Before we speak a word, He knows exactly what we'll say.

It's easy to forget this. We live in an undisciplined, go-for-the-pleasure society. We are faced with too many decisions and choices and opportunities to do things and go places. We don't stop long enough to take a good look at what's going on inside. Everybody's running, running, running; very few are stopping to ask, "*What* am I doing? *Where* am I going? *Who* am I trying to be anyway?"

You Can't Run Far Enough

But no matter where you run, you can't hide from God. Running is a state of mind. You don't even have to leave the town where you live to "run." You don't have to go to Nashville or Lamu or anywhere else. You can just run into drugs, drinking, or the occult. You can also run into a job, a career, or starting your own business. You can run into your own thoughts, daydreams, and fantasies, but you'll never run far enough to get away from God.

God actually has you surrounded—that's what the psalmist means when he says, "You hem me in—behind and before." God's hand is upon you; His hand is always on your life, no matter how bad it gets, no matter how bad you feel, or how mad you might get at God or anyone else.

No wonder David is impressed. If he were using today's jargon, he'd probably say, "This simply blows my mind. It's more than I can handle. It's just too fantastic and a lot higher than I can ever reach."

They're Shrubs, Not Bushes!

I moved to Nashville and in the process turned from a double agent into a prodigal. You may know the story of the prodigal son. In Luke's gospel Jesus tells about a young guy who wanted to leave home, go to faraway places, and live it up. He did just that, and before he was through he wasted himself . . . "on parties and prostitutes" (Luke 15:13, TLB).

I can identify. Before I was through with my crazy times in Nashville, I wasted myself, too. I skipped the prostitutes, but I didn't skip many parties.

Success didn't come overnight. In fact, success took its time. I moved in with Shane Keister's brother, Beau, who owned a landscape business. To earn rent money, I worked for Beau during the day planting shrubs. I remember that I used to call them "bushes," and Beau hated that. He would practically scream at me, "They're shrubs! They're *not* bushes. They're SHRUBS!"

Whatever . . . all I knew was that every shrub meant digging a good-sized hole in the humid Nashville heat. That summer I think I sweated enough to float the *Queen Mary*. Nights I wrote a little music, working with Shane's wife, Alice, who was a songwriter for Paragon, a publisher of Christian music in Nashville. But I'm afraid I did more partying than songwriting.

That September I struck what seemed like pure gold to me. I became a "club man," playing in a club band in the night-clubs around Nashville. I was making three bills a week, and that was awesome to me.

I also started living with a drug dealer. I didn't know he dealt drugs when I moved from Beau's place into his. I met him in a club, and he liked the way I played. He and his wife needed some help with the rent, and I thought I needed a change of scene.

I soon learned the scene was bad. My new landlord was dealing to just about everybody in town with any drug you'd care to name. But by then I was into the Nashville nightlife and smoking pot on a regular basis. I didn't ever go into drugs in a big way, but I thought I could play around with them and get away with it. At the time, I didn't know how wrong I could be. The first lines of "Lamu" describe how messed up my head really was:

> And when it's right—Lamu nights . . . they can be so inviting . . . heaven here on earth . . . But I hear you telling me . . . this is every-thing you need . . .

Those Short-Lived Nashville Nights

Those "Nashville nights" playing in the clubs seemed like heaven on earth for somebody who had been bored out of his skull in music theory classes back in college. I was trying to fill the void, and for a while it seemed to work. But my job with the club band lasted only three months, and by November I was out of work and running short of money. I moved in with my younger sister, Kim, who had also moved to Nashville by then.

In December I hooked on with a country singer and played with him in clubs for a few weeks, but that soon ended. As 1979 began, I took a job at a Coca-Cola bottling plant. Every few days the machine would break and glass would fly in every direction, especially into my bare hands. I kept looking at my cut fingers and thinking, *Man, I can't play the piano without these.*

But I stuck it out for a few months at least. Somehow I got a credit card. I loved to take my friends out and say, "Dinner's on me, man." Pretty soon I was in the hole over two thousand dollars and almost always broke.

If my folks hadn't sent me twenty-five dollars now and then, I would have gone hungry a lot more often. My grocery shopping included crackers, baloney, and eight "mini-Millers." And that's how I survived, on Miller beer, lots of crackers and baloney, and an occasional pizza when I could afford it. It was a miserable, frustrating time for me. I was a full-time prodigal—a real backslider as they say in my church. But no matter how frustrated I got, I still believed with all my heart that God really had a plan for my life and that He still wanted to use me.

I must have been just about the weirdest combination you could find. Here I was—miserable, in debt, eating junk food, getting high, feeling guilty, praying, and talking to people about Jesus even when I was high—all at the same time! The rest of that next verse in "Lamu" describes me well:

```
. . . the way you feel isn't real . . . You
attempt to try and fill . . . the void that's
digging thru . . . and it's killing you when you
run to . . . Lamu—far away . . .
```

In October 1979, I left the Coca-Cola plant to hook on with another club band, but that only lasted for a little over a month. Then I had to hustle a dollar wherever I could—waiting tables and clerking in a clothing store.

Break Me, God

I was in the dumps and desperate, but two things kept working on me. As messed up as I was, I still believed that God had a call on my life and that I was supposed to fill that call.

Oh, I knew God was there, all right. David's words in Psalm 139 fit me like a glove:

> Where can I go from your Spirit? Where can I flee from your presence? If I go up to the heavens, you are there; if I make my bed in the depths, you are there . . . If I say, "Surely the darkness will hide me and the light become night around me," even the darkness will not be dark to you; the night will shine like the day, for darkness is as light to you. (Ps. 139:7–8, 11–12, NIV)

I totally understand how David could write Psalm 139, being in love with God one minute and wanting to hide from Him the next. I was trying to hide in the shadows and darkness of Nashville's nightlife, but I still kept praying that God would break me. I actually asked Him to make me miserable. I asked Him to do whatever He had to do—break my legs, if necessary—to turn me around.

Finally one night, while I was alone in the apartment, God put the finishing touches on answering my prayers. I guess I had a mini nervous breakdown right there on the kitchen floor. I was out of a job, broke, hungry, and miserable. I had no peace. I was lonely, a failure—and very tired of crackers and baloney.

I started crying and, for the first time in years, I came really clean with God. I'd played double agent, and then I'd played the prodigal, and now, just like the prodigal son in the Bible, I "came to [my] senses" (Luke 15:17, NIV) and realized there was only one way out of my pig pen. I had to go back to my heavenly Father. I can remember saying, "God, I can't do it by myself and right now I'm willing to make a turn."

And that was it. I can't explain why I didn't pray that simple prayer a long time before I did. I guess I was too proud or too messed up to think straight. I always felt guilty. I always had lots of remorse and self-pity, but I couldn't—or wouldn't—*repent* and really make the turn until that night in the apartment.

God Finally Got through to Me

There is no way to run from God when He is inside of you, and He had been part of my life since I was ten years old. Scripture says that as Christians our body becomes the temple of the Holy Spirit (see 1 Cor. 6:19). For the first time I clearly saw Satan had a real hold on me. I realized what kind of spiritual warfare was going on between my old and new natures.

Of course, it wasn't all Satan's doing. I had done plenty to mess things up myself by experimenting with marijuana and alcohol. I'd been cocky, proud, careless, and stupid. Without God's intervention, there would have been *no way* for me to have gotten out of the trap.

Ever since my junior year in high school, I had been grieving the Holy Spirit, ignoring His soft, gentle voice that kept telling me to "turn around, come on back home." But the Holy Spirit is never pushy. I was free to choose not to let Him have control or to let Him give me life and peace (see Rom. 8:6).

My turnaround was the most painful thing I have ever been through. If I'd known how painful it was going to be, I probably would never have prayed so hard to have it happen! I thought I could run to some kind of "Lamu" far away and put my pain behind me, but the pain came right along with me:

```
. . . because you never can run . . . from the
one inside of you.
```

It doesn't matter where you try to run. The only real traveling you do is in your mind and your soul. You can run to whatever Lamu you like—an island, a resort, your local hangout, drugs, or booze—losing yourself in having good times. Or you can really repent, turn around, and stop wanting to do things your way without God. You can come home to the Father. He is always ready and waiting to welcome you back!

4

Don't Believe Everything You Hear

You may have heard the story of the two frogs who were swimming around in a big kettle of water. One of them said, "My, isn't this water nice and warm?"

"Yes," said the other, "this is great. Let's just float around in here forever."

And so the two frogs just kicked back and relaxed, not realizing that every few minutes the heat was being turned up under the kettle ever so slightly and the water was getting hotter and hotter. And before they knew what had happened, they were totally cooked and ready to become somebody's lunch.

Of course, this is just a crazy little story. But something very similar really did happen a few years ago to a couple sitting in a hot tub. Somehow, the heat got turned up too high and both of them failed to notice that the water was getting dangerously hot. They were both found dead—parboiled in their own hot tub!

Frogs or people getting cooked without knowing it—what's the point?

A Hot Tub Called "The System"

We live in a secular society that I call "The System." In a lot of ways The System is just like a hot tub that is getting too hot. We are slowly getting cooked in water that seems comfortable, but it's killing us spiritually.

Twenty-four hours a day The System pounds us with one message: "Live it up. Go for the pleasure. That's what life is all about!" We did a song to describe what's going on everywhere in a world that's "Wired for Sound."

The world's sounds are:

```
Comin' on like a tidal wave . . . That washes
thru the brain—a state of mind . . . No dispute
when the noise is made . . . And so it lets the
blind lead the blind . . . Lured by charisma to
be swayed to believe.
```

"Wired for Sound" is a pretty accurate description of the world we live in. With a flick of a switch or the twist of a knob we can turn on just about any kind of entertainment we want. We even talk about being "turned on" or "turned off," meaning, "Yeah, I really liked that," or "It was pathetic—really lame—a loser."

It's perfectly natural to judge a record, a TV show, or a video by how it turns us on or off, but it's not always easy to know if it's good or bad. Some stuff is obviously straight from The Pit, but a lot of other things are a mix of good, not so good, and just plain "hard to tell."

One thing is sure. A great deal of what is on TV, the radio, records, and films is very, very attractive. The people performing in all these media have charisma and power that are beyond imagination. They can start styles, change public opinion, and even elect presidents. They influence thousands by simply singing a song, cutting a record, or appearing on a talk show.

Who Is Really Right?

The chorus of "Wired for Sound" focuses on a very crucial idea: Today everyone can be an expert or an authority. What is true? What is right? What is honest? Who knows? We live in a world where all truth is relative—meaning "my truth or what I think is right is just as good as yours, as long as it works for me." There is no absolute or final truth.[1]

Word of mouth is the counselor . . . there is
no need for proof . . . in a world that's wired
for sound . . . the tongue becomes the mighty
sword . . . that battles the truth . . . in a
world that's wired for sound.

"Wired for Sound" is saying everything is *not* relative. One opinion is not necessarily as good as another. Yes, of course, everyone has a right to his or her own opinion, and in that sense, one person's ideas deserve as much respect as another person's. But that doesn't mean everyone's opinion is correct, healthy, or even safe. How, then, can you decide? What standard do you use?

I believe you have to use one very special opinion that is higher, better, and more correct than all the others in the world. I'm talking about God's opinion. He's the One who created the world in the first place, and He sent His Son to redeem the world from sin. God's truth is not relative to anything. His truth is absolute.

But God does not dictate or force His truth on anyone. You are free to make up your own mind. You can listen to sounds designed to serve God, or you can listen to sounds designed to serve Satan. That's what Paul was talking about when he wrote to Christians in the first century:

Our struggle is not against flesh and blood, but . . .
against the powers of this dark world and against
the spiritual forces of evil in the heavenly realms.
(Eph. 6:12, NIV)

The reason The System is capable of slowly cooking us is that Satan is in charge of this world (see Eph. 2:2). He got promoted to "ruler" of the world when Adam and Eve first sinned. That's why God sent His Son to open our eyes and turn us from darkness to light (see Acts 26:18).

Before that "turnaround night" in my Nashville apartment, I knew the difference between darkness and light, but I was playing around in the shadows, trying to worship God and fool with The System, too. I was wired for sound, all right, and my wires were totally crossed. It made me so miserable I couldn't stand it, and I repented, confessed, and asked God to forgive me.

I know *repented* is an old-fashioned word, but it needs to be taken more seriously, especially when The System has so many attractions that can really foul up your life. It's one thing to feel bad about sin. You can even be miserable with remorse, but repenting means you decide to turn away from what you've been doing and go in a completely new direction. The word the Bible uses for repentance literally means "to change your mind," and that's exactly what I decided to do that night when I gave in and asked God to take over.

God, Please Rewire My Mind

I didn't whip out a Bible the next morning and read Romans 12:1–2 aloud, but I did start trying to live according to what it says:

And so, dear brothers and sisters, I plead with you to give your bodies to God. Let them be a living and **holy sacrifice**—the kind he will accept. When you think of what he has done for you, is this too much to ask? Don't copy the behavior and customs of this world, but let God transform you into a new person by changing the way you think. Then you will know what God wants you to do, and you will know how good and pleasing and perfect his will really is. (Romans 12: 1–2, NLT)

I really wanted what Paul describes in verse 2. The world (The System) had been squeezing me into its own mold—and also cooking me in its own hot tub—but I wanted God to do a job on my mind and rewire it according to His will.

It's funny, but when you decide to change, it often happens that your "luck" changes, too. I know what I'm about to tell you will sound like one of those "likely stories" you might hear on TV talk shows, but it's true.

The same day that I started over I visited Paragon Company to see what was going on. Whatever songs I was writing at the time I would play for them. Paragon had published only two or three of my songs up until then. They liked my music but told me as kindly as they could that my lyrics didn't fly too high.

When I walked into Paragon that day, Randy Cox, the publisher, said, "Hey, I want to talk to you. This group called 'Higher Ground' needs a piano player. You need to consider it."

So I met the guys from "Higher Ground." They did concerts all over the southern states. They offered me $125 a week to play piano and keyboard and do a little singing. I took the job.

We hit the road, and I was with the group for nine months. It was a great life! I started reading the Bible and had devotional times with the band as well as with people we met where we played. We didn't just minister to them—they ministered to us!

I Belonged

Those nine months gave me some of the best memories of my life. It was where I needed to be at that time. I needed that support from solid, mature Christians who could help me get my head straight and become what Scripture calls "a new and different person with a fresh newness in all you do and think" (Rom. 12:2, TLB).

Eventually, I left "Higher Ground" and went on to writing songs and making albums. But we still try to communicate the message of Romans 12:2. We realize that the tongues of certain secular rock stars have been the wrong kind of "counselor" to millions of kids and that their "word of mouth" often is all that's needed to convince kids about the way to live.

We know that a lot of you are being asked to believe a lot of lies. These tongues are mighty swords that are battling against God's truth every way they can. As "Wired for Sound" says, it's:

```
easier believing what is hard to get rid of
than to try . . . Never searching—just
accepting . . . Feeds the mind enough to get
you by . . . Scratching the surface yet to dig
deeper down.
```

Satan never wants us to dig any deeper than "Is it fun? Does it feel good? Is it good for laughs? Can I forget my pressures and troubles for just a little while?"

If those are the only questions we ask, it's easy to be lulled into thinking, "The System is the cool, sophisticated, hip way to live." Or you can make the mistake I made and try to "serve both sides." You may try to say the right things for the church crowd and then the right things for the secular crowd that prefers The System.

I was fooled for a while myself, and it almost destroyed my life. But I started asking harder questions and started digging deeper into who I really was and who God really was to me. Who was I trying to please—a certain group of people or Him? It always comes down to that.

Please Him, Please Yourself

It's funny, though, if you please Him, you'll not only please yourself but also all the people God has put in your life for your good. If you use God's wisdom and standards to think for yourself, you may offend some people. You may lose some friends. But are they friends worth having? Are they really friends if they won't accept you unless you buy into the lifestyle of The System, which emphasizes a "craze for sex, the ambition to buy everything that appeals to you, and the pride that comes from wealth and importance" (1 John 2:16, TLB)?

I get some criticism for being part of the rock-'n'-roll scene, which some well-meaning Christians believe automatically puts us "on the side of the devil." I'm sorry they feel that way, but we know whose side we are really on, and it's definitely not Satan's. Every week I get letters and phone calls from kids who tell me, "You saved my life . . . You got me going in the right direction . . . Because of your songs I got off drugs . . . I'm back on track spiritually . . . God is close again."

We know from the mail we receive that songs like "You're Alright" and "The Last Letter" have helped a lot of kids out of the despondency that leads to suicide. And we've received letters from many girls who say that "Old Enough to Know" was written directly to help them resist the pressures they are facing to have sex before marriage with somebody who claims to "love" them.

Following the release of *The Big Picture* album, we got a letter from a music major named Joe who said: "Your music gets right to the heart . . . I have been drawn closer to the Lord as a result of your ministry."

Lisa wrote:

> Your example showed that you can have fun and still be serious about your faith. . . . Your music has real meaning.

A younger teenage girl named Jenny wrote to say she hadn't been feeling very close to Jesus:

> I got your record this summer and it was almost like being introduced to Him. . . . A million thank-yous for sharing your talents and helping me see Christ in my life.

Chuck bought our "In Concert" video and wrote later to tell us: "For the past few years I've been struggling with a lot of doubts . . . As you recited Psalm 139, something inside of me snapped. The sudden realization that the Lord is always with me and that there is no way I can hide from Him really hit me."

We talked with Kris after a concert, and she wrote later to say:

> It seems as though through my many struggles and trials in life, God has used your music. It has reached to the deepest parts of my heart and touched the hardness or hurt hiding there, to show me a glimpse of Him and His love. I support and back you up because of the realness I have seen in you.

We Want to Make a Difference for God

I don't share these letters with you to take some kind of ego trip. I want to give you a small taste of the dramatic difference God is making in lives. Nobody can tell me my music is from the devil when I see someone's life changed for the good. The devil is only interested in changing a person's life for the bad. I can vouch for that.

We want to give an alternative to anyone willing to plug into a sound that is for the truth and for positive things. As "Wired for Sound" says, *Wisdom from the sacred page is turned and ignored.* We want our music to cause people to turn to the sacred pages of Scripture and let God change their lives.

Before He left this world, Jesus promised to send the Comforter—the Holy Spirit—who would teach us all things and guide us into all truth (see John 14:26; 16:13). As you turn to God's wisdom on the sacred pages of Scripture, the Holy Spirit will remake your life from the inside. If you're like me, you need these quiet times often. You need to get away from the world that is "wired for sound"—the phone, the TV, headphones, the radio, etc.—and just spend time with Him. He's the answer to the noise and the distractions.

Do you want the kind of self-esteem that can say no to The System? Then start to take control of the sounds that bombard your mind. The world is wired for sound, but you are in control of the "on" switch and the volume. Don't listen to and watch "just anything." Don't believe everything you see and hear. Test it with God's wisdom and become a new and different person!

5

Go for It!

Ken Abraham, a drummer for a Christian rock group called "Abraham," got on a 6:00 A.M. flight out of a midwestern city headed for New York. He was just settling into a window seat when he was joined by a handsome couple. The man was dressed in a tux, the woman in a red evening dress.

The couple introduced themselves as Bill and Jennifer. Ken wasn't quite sure what to say, so he asked, "Going some place special?"

Jennifer bubbled, "We sure are! We won a three-day trip to Nassau last night!"

They had won the trip the night before at a promotional drawing held by a local radio station in a popular restaurant. The only entrance requirement was that each couple had to bring a packed suitcase and literally be ready to leave on the trip right then if they won.

Because Jennifer and Bill thought they couldn't possibly win, they didn't pack much in the suitcase. But sure enough, they had come up winners! They caught the plane, with strict instructions to take only what they had in their suitcase.

"I guess we'll have to wear the clothes we have on our backs," laughed Bill. "I don't even have any money to buy anything once we get there."

So, there they were, on a 6:00 A.M. flight, headed for the Bahamas, with just a few dollars in their pockets and an empty suitcase. But did they care? They thought it was a "nice joke."[1]

Living with an "Empty Suitcase"

There is a real picture here of the way a lot of people live from day to day—on the "empty suitcase" principle. They don't have any goals. They don't make any preparations, and they don't have anything packed. Because they're really not ready to get anyplace in life, they seldom do.

I've met high schoolers and collegians who make more plans for a big prom night or their graduation party than they do for the rest of their lives. They often wind up sitting on the sidelines, letting The System squeeze them a little more each day as they try to make it to Friday so they can have a "great weekend."

At the other extreme, some people believe that setting goals and making plans don't mix with having "real faith in God." Somehow having goals and plans sounds as if you're self-centered, doing things on your own, and ignoring God's will for your life. I can't agree, however, because the Bible is full of teachings on setting goals and making plans that are *motivated by the right Source.*

Solomon, one of the wisest men who ever lived, wrote: "All a man's ways seem innocent to him, but motives are weighed by the LORD. Commit to the LORD whatever you do, and your plans will succeed" (Prov. 16:2–3, NIV). He also said, "We should make plans—counting on God to direct us" (Prov. 16:9, TLB).

Did Jesus Have Goals?

Jesus was the greatest goal setter of them all. He said he came not to abolish the law and the prophets but "to fulfill them" (Matt. 5:17, NIV). He said He hadn't come to be served but to serve others and to give His life "as a ransom for many" (Matt. 20:28, NIV), and to "seek and to save what was lost" (Luke 19:10, NIV). Jesus said He didn't come to judge the world, but to save it (see John 12:47) and to give us far more life than we've ever had before (see John 10:10).

Everything Jesus did was motivated by His heavenly Father. If we want to follow Christ, our motivation has to be the same. Solomon also said, "We can make our plans, but the final outcome is in God's hands. We can always 'prove' that we are right, but is the Lord convinced?" (Prov. 16:1–2, TLB).

Sometimes we try to convince God we're doing His will, but He knows us far better than we do. He knows if we really want to pay the full price to serve and follow Him.

That's what we're trying to get across in the first verse of "Pursuit of the Dream":

Wake up and dream about . . . the plans you have in store for you . . . but keep in mind . . . it's not just what you do . . . but what you do it for—and who . . . There are roads to discover . . . There are stories yet to be told . . . as you see the big picture . . . just beginning to unfold.

Stay or Launch Out?

I spent nine months out on the road with "Higher Ground," discovering new roads and trying to get a better grasp on the big picture for my life. I began to wonder how long I should stay in this safe, comfortable niche, walking closely with God and having a great time playing and singing.

And then a new offer came. Would I be interested in a one-year contract to write songs for Paragon at two hundred dollars a week? I first had to examine my motives. Was I just going for the pay raise and the glamour? After all, I would get two hundred dollars a week just to hang out and write songs all day. It was what I'd always dreamed of, but was it what God had in mind?

The chorus of "Pursuit of the Dream" describes the kind of line I was trying to walk:

> So, break down the barriers . . . but don't bend the rules . . . Never forget your roots . . . as you head for something new . . . Ride thru the shades of desire . . . letting the light be seen . . . and He'll steer the heart in the . . . pursuit of the dream.

I knew there were plenty of barriers ahead and dangers, too. To go with Paragon meant being back on my own—living in Nashville with no more daily support from the other guys in "Higher Ground." There would be temptations to drift a little, sell out to a desire for fame and fortune. Was I ready for the test? I thanked God for my roots. I knew I wanted to live a godly life, but had I grown up enough to let Him steer my heart completely?

I was at a crossroads, and I decided to go for it—not in a crazy, reckless way, but with real purpose. I had learned to listen to the Lord. Whatever I did, it was always on one condition: "Lord, if this isn't where I should be, You let me know it in a big way."

So I made the leap and pursued my dream to be a songwriter and musician who would reach the world with his music. Now I see clearly it was the best decision I ever made. But back then I couldn't know for sure. I had to trust God and take it a step at a time.

Because I was green and inexperienced, writing for Paragon was a struggle for a while. I wrote a lot of stuff they couldn't use, but I also learned a lot about what did work.

Things really started to come together. I met Amy Grant and started doing some songs with her. I met and married my wife, Debbie, and three days after our wedding, I signed a three-year contract as a songwriter. In 1982, I joined Amy's tour group, and within the next two years, I recorded two albums of my own.

Always Ask Two Questions

Over these last few years we've had the privilege of sharing our music and our faith with thousands of kids and young adults. And it all started with my decision to "go for it" when I was offered a chance to write songs for Paragon Publishing Company. But I had a purpose—a goal worth going for, and that's exciting. I try to test my goals to see if they are worthwhile to God as well as to me. I always ask two questions: (1) Am I being true to God? and (2) Am I being true to myself—the kind of person God made me to be?

To be true to God and yourself you need to know where your boundaries are—not limitations or things to hold you back but God's rules and principles to live by. God deals more in guidelines than in a lot of "dos and don'ts." They're summed up in the commandment Jesus said was most important: "'Love the Lord your God with all your heart and with all your soul and with all your mind.' This is the first and greatest commandment. And the second is like it: 'Love your neighbor as yourself'" (Matt. 22:37–39, NIV).

If you keep these two commandments, you will automatically keep all the others that talk about not lying, stealing, coveting, and having sex outside of marriage. As you pursue your dream, you won't need somebody holding your hand and telling you if something is right or wrong.

Instead simply ask yourself if what you're going for helps you love God and your neighbor (meaning everyone from your family and friends to coaches and teachers). Answer these questions honestly, and you will always know when you are starting to compromise your commitment to Christ and the Scriptures. Remind yourself: "These are the rules. I will not compromise on these issues. This is what I'm all about." One of my favorite passages of Scripture is Psalm 37:4–5:

> Delight yourself also in the LORD, and He shall give you the desires of your heart. Commit your way to the LORD, trust also in Him, and He shall bring it to pass. (NKJV)

Those are two great verses to memorize as you pursue any dream you might have. When you commit your life to Him and really trust Him, He will make things happen that you never dreamed of. He will use you in powerful and amazing ways.

Pursuing Any Dream Takes Work

But it's a trade-off. You just don't sit around praying, "Lord, do wonderful things in my life and make my dreams come true." Pursuing anything takes work and effort.

I got a letter from Diana who is pursuing a twenty-seven-second 220-yard dash as she competes on the girls' track team at school. She realizes she wasn't running to her full potential last year and that she was clashing with her coach. Then she adds,

Most of it is that I wasn't running for Jesus' glory but for my glory, and I found out that doesn't work out at all. When I was at camp this last summer, I made a commitment to be gutsy for God. I meant it! I want to give Jesus all the glory in track this year. I know that a 27-second 220 will be most definitely hard, but I can do it. . . . That's my dream in track. That's why I love your song because I'm in my pursuit of a dream.

Whether Diana runs a 27-second 220 or has to settle for 28 seconds isn't the most important thing. What counts is that she has decided to commit herself to God and get "gutsy" for Him. If she's trusting in Him, He will bring to pass in her life what He wants to happen.

It's always good to remember that while we may want to pursue our dream, God may have something else in mind. It's easy to dream a big dream and think, *Oh, this is what God wants me to do.* Then if it doesn't happen, you think God tricked you or you fouled up and God's judging you. Whenever you pursue your dream, it's always a matter of stopping long enough to reflect on what God wants you to do.

Knowing you're being true to God and doing what He wants is exciting and energizing, and being true to God always leads to being true to yourself. You can relax and not worry about being somebody you aren't and chasing dreams that you know aren't yours.

I appreciate Kimberly's letter, which says:

> Your song "Pursuit of the Dream" is probably the most special to me. It seems like everyone and even Grandma's dog has some big ideas about what you should do with your life—who you should be—teachers push, parents push. People don't understand that it's OK for me to be a mother and a wife—or a writer—or a piano teacher. Being high school valedictorian doesn't mean your name has to be on the med school roster. It's nice to know there's someone out there who is actually encouraging me to do what I want to do—to go after my dreams—as long as I remember who I'm going to do it for!

Filling in the "Big Picture"

I think Kimberly has a good handle on what we like to call the "big picture." The second verse of "Pursuit of the Dream" says:

> It's all right to find yourself . . . thinking now and then . . . about the way you want your life to be . . . anticipating what lies . . . just around the bend . . . Can't wait to see . . . Comes the time of decision . . . Some you dodge and some you should face . . . As you

see the big picture . . . there will be some dues
to pay.

Seventeen-year-old Lynn wrote to say:

> I have a problem I think you can help me with. I
> want to get to know God like you know God. But
> how? How do I learn how to love God? I believe
> in Him, but I just don't know Him. I feel that if I
> know God I'll know who I am inside. I want to love
> Him. Please help me! I need God in my life, what's
> life without Him?

I'm flattered that Lynn wants to get to know God like I know Him, but I hope she can go way beyond that. I'm still working on getting to know God better myself! That's what the "big picture" is all about—knowing God personally, wanting to do His will, and realizing that life is nothing without Him.

Knowing God personally is a pretty tall order for a goal. It could seem so unreachable that you might be tempted to give up before you begin. Instead of trying to fill in the whole picture all at once, set some smaller, more specific goal that will fill in a corner of the picture. And set a specific date for reaching that goal. Maybe it's something as simple as deciding you're going to spend fifteen minutes a day every day for the next month reading the Bible and praying. Tackle just that much. Then, as soon as you have filled in that corner, move on to the next goal—just a little farther out. Bit by bit, you'll be filling in the "big picture" and getting to know God better.

Wayne Kirkpatrick, who wrote the lyrics for "Pursuit of the Dream," believes we are all filling in the "big picture" throughout our lives. We are always discovering more of God's perfect will as we move through His process of maturing us, as we pursue the dream with Him. As the last verse of the song says:

Wake up and dream about . . . the plans you have in store for you . . . but keep in mind . . . it's not just what you do . . . but what you do it for—and who . . . There are choices that build you . . . choices that will make you fall . . . all part of the big picture . . . One day you will see it all.

I love what Paul wrote in Philippians 3:12–14. Paul knew he wasn't perfect, that he hadn't learned everything. But he kept working toward that day when he could finally be all that Christ saved him to be. Paul said, "I am still not all I should be but I am bringing all my energies to bear on this one thing: Forgetting the past and looking forward to what lies ahead, I strain to reach the end of the race and receive the prize for which God is calling us up to heaven because of what Christ Jesus did for us" (Phil. 3:13–14, TLB).

What I hear Paul saying is that Christ is our goal and our guide as we pursue our dreams. He's telling us to go for it!

chapter six

The Hardest Word You'll Ever Say

C athy's letter speaks for a lot of teenagers who are struggling with saying the hardest word of all:

> You know at this age things start to move in life where your friends try to talk you into things that you know aren't right and that are unpleasing to the Lord. Your older boyfriend tries to talk you into sex. That sort of thing. Well, I had this guy that I really liked a lot, but he was two years older than I was. I didn't feel that having a relationship with him was a good idea because I could be pressured into something that I knew was wrong . . . I decided the best thing to do was say no. A little while after that, I wondered if I made the right choice or not. But the song "You're Alright" let me know that I did the right thing for myself and for the Lord. Michael, each one of your songs has helped me decide what I need to do for the Lord and how to get back on track with Him. They've helped me to say no to my friends and to take a stand for Jesus. I'm really thankful!

I'm impressed by Cathy's letter because she knows the cost—and the value—of saying no! When you say no to special people like boyfriends and they don't like it, your self-esteem can be very vulnerable. As Cathy says, "The question comes to mind if I made the right choice or not."

How can you be sure you're making the right choice? As I

mentioned in chapter four, everybody has an opinion and, of course, everybody thinks his or her opinion is right. Cathy's boyfriend thinks it would be right to have sex with her. Why? *Because he wants the pleasure.* His "standards" really don't go any farther than that.

Arguments from friends can sound convincing when you don't stick to standards that are solid and unchanging. But, when you can remember the truth from God's Word, you know when you "do the right thing."

From "You're Alright" to "Strong and Courageous"

"You're Alright" is a song to help you when you're on the defensive, but what about going on the offense and moving out with confidence to say no to the evil stuff? That's when you need to be "strong and courageous," which is the theme of a song on my first album, *Michael W. Smith Project.*

"Be Strong and Courageous" is a very high energy tune, matched up with words based on the first eleven verses of the first chapter of Joshua. It has one simple message: To be strong and courageous you have to keep reading, studying, and practicing God's Word. If you know what He says and you do it, you'll be able to handle life successfully, including all those times when you have to say no.

At the time God told Joshua to be strong and courageous, Joshua needed all the help he could get. Moses had just died, and Joshua had been promoted to commander in chief of Israel's armies, which were camped on the banks of the Jordan, waiting to be led into battle to gain the promised land on the other side of the river.

Any time you think about pursuing your dream to bring

God some glory, you're in the same boat Joshua was. The first verse of "Be Strong and Courageous" sets the scene:

> My servant now your time has come . . . you have a job to do . . . I have a people to be led . . . and a willing heart in you . . . So I give you strength and courage . . . and I'll hide you in My hand . . . For Joshua, you gotta live for your call . . . Take My people to their land.

Joshua Faced Heavy Odds

If you're up on your Old Testament history, you know that "taking God's people to their land" meant a little more than putting them on a ferry and crossing over to stay at the Jordan Hilton. Canaan's borders weren't unfamiliar. The Israelites had been there once before, but lack of faith kept them from going in. God sentenced them to forty more years of wandering.

Now they were back. Moses had climbed Mount Nebo, and God had taken him to his last resting place. Then God chose Joshua to lead His people against the fortified cities of Canaan, defended by well-trained warriors equipped with iron chariots. To conquer Canaan, Joshua and his troops would have to go up against the giant sons of Anak, the Canaanites, *and* six other nations, all greater and mightier than Israel. But God told Joshua not to worry, but to listen to His encouragement and advice:

> No one will be able to stand up against you all the days of your life. As I was with Moses, so I will be

with you; I will never leave you nor forsake you. Be strong and courageous, because you will lead these people to inherit the land I swore to their forefathers to give them.

Be strong and very courageous. Be careful to obey all the law my servant Moses gave you; do not turn from it to the right or to the left, that you may be successful wherever you go. Do not let this Book of the Law depart from your mouth; meditate on it day and night, so that you may be careful to do everything written in it. Then you will be prosperous and successful. Have I not commanded you? Be strong and courageous. Do not be terrified; do not be discouraged, for the LORD your God will be with you wherever you go. (Joshua 1:5–9, NIV)

Joshua was a seasoned warrior who had fought many battles under Moses' command. But now God has to tell him to be "strong and courageous" *three times*. Obviously, Joshua is afraid, and who can blame him? He doesn't have as many men. He has no iron chariots, and he will have to attack cities whose walls are thirty feet thick and over thirty feet high. But God doesn't plan on bringing in reinforcements and better equipment. He prefers to give Joshua two more important things: the freedom to fail and a "guarantee" to avoid failure.

Why Are We Afraid to Fail?

Nobody likes failure. It's easier not to try than to risk being humiliated or embarrassed. Stop for a minute and think about why you get frustrated and why you have fears. Don't they come from wanting something very badly? After all, you might lose your reputation or your popularity. Isn't your pride in there somewhere, too?

God gave Joshua freedom to fail by encouraging him and bolstering his faith. There were no threats or hints of what would happen to Joshua if he were defeated by the Canaanites. God wanted Joshua to be willing to try because he trusted Him. He wanted Joshua to realize that it is never a case of "having to succeed"; it's always a case of being obedient.

There's a great old story about an SOS call coming into a Coast Guard station from a ship going down on the rocks just off the coast of South Carolina. As the SOS call comes in, the young seaman looks out at the roaring waves and says, "We can't go out in this. We'll never get back!" But then the old captain of the rescue team says, "We have to go out. We don't have to come back."

Maybe that sounds a little dramatic, but it says something about having the freedom to fail. The captain knew he had to try to save the sailors who were going down. Whether or not he succeeded was up to God. He wasn't afraid to fail.

Trusting Is Easier Said than Done

Scripture teaches that God loves us with a perfect love and "perfect love drives out fear" (1 John 4:18, NIV). Why? Because when you talk about fear, you're talking about punishment, and as long as you're in God's love you don't face punishment anymore. You don't have to fear failure because you don't *have* to be successful. You simply have to make a decision to follow God and trust that His plans will be accomplished.

It's easy to say but not as easy to do. I got a taste of this myself in 1982, when I started touring with Amy Grant and her band. In her first tour early that year, I played keyboard and sang a little. I was also writing songs for Amy and writing a few things of my own.

Mike Blanton and Dan Harrell, Amy's managers, liked my music and became my managers as well. They kept encouraging me to think about doing my own album as soon as I was ready. One day I played a new song for Mike called "You Need a Savior." I had done the music and my wife, Debbie, had done the lyrics. Mike said, "Bring me seven or eight other songs like that, and we'll cut a record."

Debbie and I went to work—she on the lyrics and I on the music—and we came up with seven other songs.

Mike told me, "I think you're ready. It's time we made an album, and I think you should probably produce it yourself."

I gulped on that one. I had written lots of songs in my life, but I had never actually produced a record before. I decided to go for it, and we produced the album in August and September. Later that fall I went back out on tour with Amy and was given the opportunity to "open" for her at each concert. To open for the main attraction is a big responsibility. You are there to warm up the audience and get them ready for the main performance.

The first time I opened for Amy we were in Lubbock, Texas. I was scared to death and thought my heart would literally stop beating. I prayed I wouldn't trip over my own feet as I moved carefully around the stage singing four songs from the *Project* album. When it was over, I was totally exhausted. I thought I had blown it, but somehow the crowd loved it and wanted more. I was shocked. I can't say that I felt particularly strong and courageous. "Relieved and grateful" would be more accurate.

During the rest of that fall tour, I struggled with my own insecurity, but Amy kept encouraging me to "just be myself." By the end of the tour, I was feeling a lot more comfortable with the crowds. Honestly, for once in my life I had the freedom to fail, and I was able to relax—and, of course, then I did much better.

Does God Give Us a Blank Check?

Along with freedom to fail, God gives us a "guarantee" for success. He told Joshua, "Do not let this Book of the Law depart from your mouth; meditate on it day and night, so that you may be careful to do everything written in it. Then you will be prosperous and successful" (Josh. 1:8, NIV).

Was God giving Joshua a blank check? Was He saying he could do whatever he liked and he'd still win every battle because he was on God's side? I don't think so. I think He was telling Joshua to let the Word of God make a difference in his life.

The second verse of "Be Strong and Courageous" says:

> Never should you fear My call . . . just listen and obey . . . Discouragement need never fall . . . stand on the words I say . . . You know I led your fathers here . . . and you know I'll lead you, too . . . Inscribe My Law into your soul . . . and nothing will touch you.

I know from experience that when you start using the Word of God in your life, you can defeat Satan every time. But if you don't use it, you'll go down and you'll land hard. Joshua found that out, too, at the Battle of Ai, when one of his soldiers got greedy (see Josh. 7).

"Using the Word" means more than just reading the Bible or even attending church and Bible studies. I did plenty of that, and I still wound up at the Flood Wall having a beer or smoking a joint and feeling guilty. Why didn't God's Word protect me? *Because I didn't put it to work in my life.* I just went through the motions. I didn't obey what God told me to do.

By the time I got to Nashville and on my own, I was into the Word less and less and into the wrong stuff more and more. Nothing changed until I was ready to make a change and to let God's Word work in my life again.

In chapter one I said that "You're Alright" is the most important song we do in every concert. But "Be Strong and Courageous" is not that far behind. The reason so many Christians lose self-esteem and start feeling worthless is that they ignore God's Word. To have a good self-image, "Do not merely listen to the word, and so deceive yourselves. Do what it says" (James 1:22, NIV).

I Struggle to Stay in the Word

I think it's a struggle for everyone—I know it is for me. Something that has really helped is reading the daily portion of *The One Year Bible,* which has the entire Bible arranged in three hundred sixty-five daily readings. The daily readings are taken from the Old Testament, the New Testament, Psalms, and Proverbs. By the end of the year, I have covered the entire Old and New Testaments, plus the Psalms twice.

Of course, I have to be consistent and read every day to

keep up. Sometimes, when I'm on the road getting from one concert to another, I fall behind. But I try to stay with it because I'm convinced that being in the Word and feeding on God's truth is one of the most important things a Christian can do each day.

When I'm not in the Word, the old nature inside is weak, the flaming arrows fly, and I can get wiped out. But when I'm in the Word—*when I write it on my heart*—then there are more victories than defeats. Then the problems aren't too heavy, and I can handle the hassles.

There is nothing magic about it. The secret is to apply what I read to my life and to what I face each day. When I let God's Word make a difference in my life, it becomes far more than words on paper, far more than rules or dry and dusty history or lectures on how to be a "goody two-shoes."

When you open your mind and heart to what the Bible is telling you, you have an open line to the Holy Spirit, who is there to teach you all truth and guide your steps. Many chapters in Scripture talk about the Holy Spirit, but my favorite is Romans 8. Here Paul tells me that I'm under no obligation to my old sinful nature. I don't have to do what it's begging me to do—the wrong thing. If I follow my old nature, I can get into deep trouble and even perish. But if I trust in the power of the Holy Spirit, I crush the old nature and its evil deeds (see Rom. 8:12–13).

Sometimes I hear kids saying, "I'll read the Bible, but it doesn't do anything for me." That's where the Holy Spirit has to come in. He is the power source. In a typical concert our sound and lighting systems can pull up to one hundred fifty thousand watts, but nothing happens if we don't plug into the main service box in the auditorium. Without power, there is no sound, no lights, no concert.

The same is true in your life. Read the Word, but also plug into the Holy Spirit, and ask Him for the power to do what it says. Then you'll know certain things are happening in your life for a reason and you will know how to handle them. God will be with you wherever you go. He will give you the strength to endure and the courage to say no.

7

You've Gotta Serve Somebody

Jesus taught that you can't serve God and money, but many people try because they think money is the way to happiness. As someone said, "It's not true that money can't buy happiness. It *can* buy happiness for about twenty minutes."[1]

We wrote a tune about a place where a lot of people go to buy happiness. When we play "Rocketown" during a concert, I often see a lot of grins and quizzical looks. I guess people wonder how I thought of that "funky" title, but when they hear what "Rocketown" is talking about, the grins turn to "knowing" looks:

A Friday night affair . . . out in the city heat . . . Always a party there . . . along the sordid street . . . And it was guaranteed . . . the place to be was Rocketown.
The drinks were two for one . . . inside the crowded bars . . . The girls would make their run . . . out on the Boulevard . . . It was the idol place . . . We lived the ways of Rocketown . . . Hang around by the street light . . . in the heart of the night life.

Everywhere we play, the crowd understands this song because every community has its "Rocketown." And if it's a large city, it has many "Rocketowns." "Rocketown" is the place where everyone is cool. They come to cruise, hang out, to look—and be looked at. There's always a party or the rumor of one.

When I was in high school and later, while I was going to college in nearby Huntington, our "Rocketown" was the

Parkette Drive-In, a hamburger and fries coffee shop on Kenova's main street. I hung out there a lot to see who was with whom, where the best parties were, and just to be seen.

I can still remember the night I was with a group of guys who definitely would not have been mistaken for part of a church choir. In walked a guy in his late twenties, who was about six years older than I was. But what made Steve Evans so familiar was that I had been a big influence in pointing him toward Christ back when I was just a sophomore in high school.

Steve was no regular hanger-on at the Parkette Drive-In, but he'd come back now and then to talk to old buddies and try to share the Lord with them. He looked at me and I looked at him. We didn't say much, but *he knew*—he knew I was definitely with the wrong crowd for the wrong reasons.

I was embarrassed, but I wasn't embarrassed enough to change—at least not that night. I was still having too good a time getting cooked by The System. I was in enemy territory, but I thought I was with friends.

At least I thought I was having a good time. "Rocketown" is that place where you go to find the bright lights and all the distractions. Of course, "Rocketown" usually delivers a lot less than it promises. Whether you have fun for twenty minutes or possibly a few hours in "Rocketown," the next morning it's a fuzzy memory, just another "full night" that turned into an empty feeling.

Who's the Hero of "Rocketown"?

When people hear "Rocketown," they get different messages. Some believe it's a parable of Christ Himself, and the next few verses certainly suggest that:

There came a certain man . . . a stranger to the crowd . . . We didn't understand . . . what He was all about . . . He walked a different pace . . . so out of place in Rocketown . . .

They made a fool of Him . . . They teased Him when he'd speak . . . But when they knocked Him down . . . He'd turn the other cheek . . . He told me I could find . . . a life outside of Rocketown . . . hang around by the street light . . . in the heart of the night life.

It's not too hard to see Jesus in lyrics like these. You certainly find Jesus walking at a different pace in the pages of the Gospels. He dealt with residents of "Rocketown" many times, but He never had fuzzy motives. He always had a clear vision of who He was and why He was there. As the chorus of "Rocketown" says:

What was His mission . . . Where was He going . . . Why was His heart light always glowing . . . All I was missing . . . He stood there holding . . . What was His secret . . . Could I know it?

The adulterous woman learned Jesus' mission when He saved her from being stoned by the Pharisees. Jesus said: "Neither do I condemn you, . . . go now and leave your life of sin" (John 8:11, NIV).

When He met the Samaritan woman at the well, He was talking to a lady who knew plenty about the "Rocketowns" of her time. Jesus told her who she was—a divorcee five times over and currently in a "living together" arrangement—and Jesus changed her life (see John 4:1–42).

I Want to Be That Stranger, Too

I believe there is another way to interpret the meaning of "Rocketown." I like to think that as I trust Christ and let the Holy Spirit control my life, I can be that certain man— a stranger to the crowd who walks at a different pace and is out of place in "Rocketown."

I was trapped by peer pressure, "Rocketowns," and partying until that night in Nashville when God grabbed me by the scruff of the neck and pointed me in the right direction. Finally, I let the Bible read me and tell me what I needed to change.

I'll never forget the first time I went back to the Parkette Drive-In in Kenova. It was the spring of 1980, and I had been out playing with "Higher Ground" for several months. I had come home for a visit, and I decided to drop in to see some of my old friends. I didn't need the action or the parties anymore. I simply wanted to see old friends and learn what had happened in their lives.

There they were—a lot of the old crowd I hung out with while going to college at Marshall, as well as some of the guys I played football with at C-K High School. I sensed it in an instant. I had changed, but they hadn't.

In no time at all, someone asked me if I'd be interested in hitting the party over at So-and-So's a little later on, but I said no. I didn't preach; I just let them know I had a different pace that was definitely out of place in "Rocketown."

Whenever I talk with my old friends, I try to share Christ in a low-key way. One thing I learned is that you don't come on strong about spiritual things to old buddies who used to hang with you at the Flood Wall or on the "Rocketown" strip. They politely listen to what Christ has done for you, but they much prefer to watch your life. That's why I go back—to show them it's possible to have peace of mind and a different pace and to remind them they have a choice, if they want to take it.

How to Handle "Rocketown"

I've shared what "Rocketown" means to me, but what should it mean to you? Like the Flood Wall, "Rocketown" is a symbol of a lifestyle. You don't have to hang out in a certain drive-in or on a certain corner. "Rocketown" can be the get-together after the game or the big party at Rhonda's house with her parents gone for the weekend. Even a trip to an amusement park with your church youth group can turn into a "Rocketown" if you have the wrong motives and attitudes. *The place* doesn't make it "Rocketown"—*the people* do.

There is nothing inherently wrong with wanting to have fun or wanting to drop in at the drive-in to see who is with whom. Being a Christian doesn't mean you have to give up good times and excitement. But being a Christian does mean you always have to understand your motives for what you're doing.

Keep in mind that for a Christian, "Rocketown" is enemy territory. You may find yourself at a party that turns into a "Rocketown" when somebody brings out a bottle or a bag and wants to "get high." When that happens, the best thing to do is get out of there fast.

If you ever are part of a "Rocketown" setting, be sure

you're there as a Christ-like influence and not because it has some kind of lure or attraction. Remember the two dogs? The old nature and the new nature inside of you are never at peace. If the old nature can use something like a "Rocketown" to lead you back into the swamp that Paul describes in Romans 7, you can be sure that's just what will happen.

But if you're following your new nature and the Holy Spirit, you will know when to avoid "Rocketown" entirely and when you can walk with that different pace as an influence for Christ.

If you want to influence "Rocketown" for the Lord, be sure you can handle it. It might be wise to take along a friend— someone who is stronger than you are. Whatever you do, don't be cocky, stupid, and reckless the way I was back in high school when I started to hang out in "Rocketown." I thought I was missing something. I thought I had to try everything. And I thought I could handle the sordid part of "Rocketown," be one of the guys, and still be a Christian.

It turned out that I didn't influence anyone. The System influenced me, and I wound up spending over three years of my life confused, guilt-ridden, frustrated, and often in a great deal of pain.

If there is anything I want to get across to Christians reading this book, it's that my years as a double agent and a prodigal were *the pits*. I know that a lot of kids who are raised in Christian homes get tired of the straight and narrow. They get bored with church and wonder if they're missing out on something by not dropping in at "Rocketown" and trying to "live a little." Please believe me, if you'll just hang in there, in the long run there are greater happiness and joy in life when you walk *with* the Lord, not *away* from Him.

Holy, Not "Holier Than Thou"

Today I can go back to "Rocketown" and try to be the influence that I wanted to be back in high school. I try to be holy, but not holier than thou. A lot of Christians are a little leery of that word *holy*. They think it means being long-faced, drab, dull, dead, no fun, etc. I understand. I had the same misconceptions until I started reading Scripture and understanding a little better the word *holy*, which is used over six hundred times in the Bible.

The definition of *holy* I like the best simply says, "being like God Himself." Peter quotes God as saying, "Be holy, because I am holy" (1 Pet. 1:16, NIV; Lev. 19:2).

But how do you live a holy life? Whenever I think of someone who is "holy," a minister I know comes to mind. He's fun and has lots of energy—a very "up" person who gets high on life. Of course, people who don't believe in Christ also can be fun and energetic. So, *holy* needs to mean some other things, too, and I see those other things in him—like his healthy respect for God, his devotion to meditating on the Word day and night, his humility, and his love for all those he contacts.

I see what Christ is doing in him, and I want that same thing happening in me. I know the Bible teaches that God already sees me as righteous because of my faith and what Christ has done on the cross (see Phil. 3:9; 1 Cor. 1:30). But if I want to become holy as He is holy, I have a lot of things that need cleaning out of my life and a lot of changes yet to be made.

And I see God working. I'm getting there. The things I did last year that were ungodly, I do less, or not at all, because I've allowed God to clean me out. But then all of a sudden, I find a whole new set of things that need dealing with. God didn't put them there; they were there all the time, but I couldn't see them because I had other things to uncover first.

When you are interested in living a holy life, you suddenly become aware of "the power of the flesh," which is just another way of describing your body and its physical appetites for food, booze, drugs, sex, power—and, of course, we can't forget money. If your appetites run the show and dominate all your decision-making, you can be sure your emotional and spiritual life will dry up fast.

It's a heavy spiritual idea, but Romans clearly teaches that sin no longer has control of us, as far as our spirits and souls are concerned. Christ has freed them from the power of sin. But sin can still run the show in our bodies if we choose to let it do so. Before you obey Christ as Savior, you have no choice. You can't do anything *but* sin. But once Jesus is your Savior and Lord, you have a choice. You are no longer a slave to sin. Now you're responsible for making a free choice to sin or to live a holy life (see Rom. 6:11–23).

My Soul Got Tied in a Knot

I see that much more clearly now than I did back when I was playing double agent and prodigal in "Rocketown." Nobody in the "Rocketown" crowd made me drink or try drugs. I chose to do it, and while my body "felt good," my soul was in a knot.

When I started hanging around with people who had bad habits, pretty soon their habits became my habits. If you look in Webster's dictionary, you'll find a definition for the word *habit* that says: "A thing done often and, hence, usually done easily; a practice or custom or act that is acquired or has become automatic."

We can choose to develop holy or unholy habits. It all depends on what we want to practice over and over again. If you're interested in holy habits, the Bible talks about training yourself in godliness (see 1 Tim. 4:7). Paul says that physical training—working out, building muscles, building your endurance, etc., is of some value, but godliness has value for *all things* (see 1 Tim. 4:8).

One thing I've learned is that it takes work and training to live a godly, holy life that is empowered by the Holy Spirit. But you can live an ungodly, unholy life with hardly any effort at all! You can develop bad habits with ease; replacing bad habits with good ones takes commitment and obedience.

You Always Serve Somebody

We all face a choice. You can serve the devil or you can serve the Lord—you always wind up serving *somebody*. The last two verses of "Rocketown" catch the feeling I had the night Steve Evans came into the Parkette Drive-In and gave me a look that said, "Michael, this is *not* the way to serve God or build holy habits."

Some didn't like Him near . . . some laughed and turned away . . . But me, I longed to hear . . . all that He had to say . . . He had a peace of mind . . . I couldn't find in Rocketown . . . and when I reached down inside me . . . I could feel the emptiness . . .

He said, it's in the heart . . . this change that comes to be . . . Now He had done His part

> . . . The choice was up to me . . . As we were standing there . . . He said a prayer for Rocketown . . . He walked off silently . . . and prayed for me . . . and Rocketown . . .

I've since gone back and apologized to Steve for that night and shared with him that I've turned it around—more correctly, God turned me around. Now I try to be that same kind of guy who has a peace of mind people can't find in "Rocketown." I want to share the change that comes to the heart when you completely open your life to Jesus Christ and serve Him and Him only.

Most people don't think twice about who they are serving when they head for "Rocketown" and party time. All they know is that they're looking for good times and some escape from pressure and reality.

There is nothing wrong with having fun and relaxing, but stop to think. You should make it "serious fun"—the kind of fun that honors God instead of insulting Him. Even when you're having fun, you gotta serve somebody!

chapter eight

Who's Your Friend?

I'd like to tell you how I met my best friend. It was March 1981, and I was sitting in a hallway outside a publisher's office waiting to go into a meeting. This cute little girl dressed in jeans passed by, and I did a double take. Our eyes met, and she smiled and went on down the hall.

A few minutes later I was still sitting there when she walked by again! This time I did a triple take and said under my breath, "I think I just saw the girl I'm going to marry."

My next thought was, *This is crazy. I don't want to get married . . . not for a few years anyway.* And then I muttered, "She must work here. I've got to find out who she is!"

Just then somebody came out and called me into my meeting. I confess I didn't pay a whole lot of attention and ended it just as soon as I could. I dashed to a telephone and called my mother. "Mom, I know you won't believe this, but I just saw the girl I'm going to marry!"

"Well, that's interesting, Michael," she said. "What's her name?"

"I don't know. I haven't met her yet. I'll call you back with all the details later."

I dashed downstairs and started asking people if they knew the cute little girl with brown hair and the shy smile. "Oh, you must mean Debbie Davis. She's new—works in shipping." I hung out for a few minutes and finally got to meet Debbie. Then we both had to get back to work, but I didn't get much done that day. Three hours later I was back and asked her for a date!

Debbie had a date that night, but I wasn't discouraged. This was the girl I was going to marry! She just didn't know it yet. The following week we had three dates in three nights, which we spent mostly talking and getting to know each other.

At the end of our third date I gave her a quick little kiss good night and said I'd call her the next day. She smiled and said that would be great. But after we parted, she cried because she knew life was changing fast, and she wasn't sure she was ready for it. She spent hours praying and asking God, "Am I really falling in love? Why, Lord, are You doing this? What about all my plans?"

As for me, I was already in love and ready to get engaged, which we did three and a half weeks after we met. Four months later we got married.

Debbie Began Writing Lyrics

I suppose some people might say we got engaged and married much too fast, but from our first date I saw that Debbie had tremendous depth and dedication to the Lord. After graduating from Wheaton College, she had spent time in Haiti working with a nutritional clinic, and she had been planning to go to the University of Tennessee to get a master's in nursing. She has always been a tremendous stabilizer in my life, truly my best friend and prayer partner.

A few months after our wedding, I discovered her ability to write poetry and lyrics. I had always dreamed of teaming up with a good lyricist. My strength was writing music. I never was too great with lyrics.

One day I found some stuff Debbie was writing, poetry mostly, and I asked her if I could read it. She said, "I guess so. It's not very good."

I read several poems and it hit me. "This is great stuff! You ought to write songs."

And that's how we started. Debbie wrote all the lyrics for

the *Michael W. Smith Project* album including "Friends," which is definitely one of my favorites.

The Story behind "Friends"

During our first year of marriage, we had a Bible study going at our house, and one of the members was Bill Jackson, who was a good friend and a vital part of our church. Bill was leaving, planning to move across the country to go to work for InterVarsity. He was coming over that evening for our last Bible study together, and we planned a little reception afterward.

"Wouldn't it be great to give Bill a special gift?" Debbie asked. "Why don't we write him a song?"

"That's a great idea," I said. Then I just blew it off and told her that we could probably write one later and send it to him. I left the room for about fifteen minutes, and when I came back, she handed me the lyrics to "Friends":

```
Packing up the dreams God planted . . . in the
fertile soil of you . . . I can't believe the
hopes He's granted . . . means a chapter in your
life is through . . . We'll keep you close as
always . . . it won't even seem you've gone . . .
'cause our hearts in big and small ways . . .
will keep the love that keeps us strong.
```

Chorus:

```
And friends are friends forever . . . if the
Lord's the Lord of them . . . and a friend will
```

not say never . . . 'cause the welcome will not end . . . Tho' it's hard to let you go . . . in the Father's hands we know . . . that a lifetime's not too long . . . to live as friends.

With the faith and love God's given . . . springing from the hope we know . . . we will pray the joy you live in . . . is the strength that now you show . . . We'll keep you close as always . . . it won't even seem you've gone . . . 'cause our hearts in big and small ways . . . will keep the love that keeps us strong.

When I read those lyrics, I was so moved I sat down and wrote a melody right then. I really have to work at a lot of tunes, but not this one. "Friends" is the kind of tune that comes along only now and then, and I'm not trying to overspiritualize when I say that I believe it was very much God-inspired.

When we sang "Friends" for Bill that night, everyone was very touched. I knew we had something on our hands. So I decided that we had to cut this song and put it on an album that would minister to a lot of people in many settings. "Friends" has been used in all kinds of ways—at funerals, memorials, in high school yearbooks, and as a graduation song for public and private schools.

Letters from My Friends

"Friends" generates more mail than any of my other songs. Often it speaks to people during a tragedy—when they have lost a good friend. For example, Trudy's letter shared that she and her husband had lost their closest and truest friend, Matthew, who was hit by a drunken driver. She said,

> "Friends" was played at his funeral and I've learned that God has a purpose for everything! . . . There were approximately three hundred young adults who attended and heard the true Word of Christ! Friends were united and relationships with Christ began!!

David, who lost his friend in a sailboat accident, wrote to say,

> Your song "Friends" was the first song I heard after he died. That was the hardest day of my life. . . . I had to face the fact that my friend, one of my best, died. I've listened to that song so much that it's starting to get worn out. . . . Thanks for letting God work through you. Something that's hard to do is letting God be my strength, but I guess that all your songs show me that God is #1.

Jessie wrote to us after she'd been to a concert and appreciated the obvious friendship among all of us in the band. Jessie's best friend was moving to another state, and she asked,

> I know Jesus is the One you're supposed to depend on, but friends, forever friends, you depend on a little bit, too. Does it ever stop hurting?

We all need and want friends very badly. When we play "Friends" in concert, I can see people everywhere embracing each other and crying as they hear this tune. This kind of thing blows me away, but it happens in just about every concert. God planned a very special relationship when He created friendship.

Friends Are Motivators

Choosing friends can be one of the most important things you ever do. Because of their powerful influence, they can be a tremendous blessing—or a real curse. I chose some wrong friends in high school. They didn't deliberately try to do me in or lead me astray, but they operated from a totally different set of values than the biblical ones that I had been taught all my life. They had the values of The System, which places emphasis on fun, pleasure, and self-centeredness. If somebody gets hurt, that's just too bad.

One of my good friends is Joe White, President of "Kanakuk-Kanakomo" Christian Sports Camps in Missouri. Every summer I take part in one of his camps and hang out with the kids and find out what's happening in their lives. Joe has written a fine book called *Friendship Pressure* in which he says that recent surveys show that the drive for friendship and acceptance is the primary motivating factor among the youth of America. Joe asks, "And why, why do so many 'best friends' rip each other off by leading each other into stuff that brings so much hurt and shame and wrecked self-image?"[1]

He quotes from a letter sent to him by a sixteen-year-old girl who said:

> When I was fifteen, I lost my most precious gift
> that I had to a football player that I did not even
> know. My best friend had set us up. She told me
> she had lost hers to the very same guy. It's been
> about a year, and so far I've willingly given myself
> to eight guys. I knew it was wrong, but I went
> ahead and did it anyway. I want to be happy and
> loved. I am so miserable because of what I have done.
> Why did my friend get me into this?[2]

There are a lot of things we could tell this girl. She didn't have to go to bed with the football player. And she didn't have to go along with being set up for that kind of situation. But the key line in her letter tells you why friends are so powerful, "I want to be happy and loved."

Everywhere you turn you can find examples of friends doing other friends in. Len Bias, a 6′8″, 230-pound Maryland basketball star, was drafted by the Boston Celtics and looked forward to a great pro career. He was with friends when he died of cardiac arrest after using cocaine. Eight days after Bias's death, Don Rogers, a twenty-seven-year-old defensive back with the Cleveland Browns, went to his own bachelor party given by friends. Roger was scheduled to be married the following day, but he didn't make it. He, too, died after using cocaine.[3]

When you think about it, people often get into trouble or do something stupid when they're with friends. As King Solomon wrote, "There are 'friends' who pretend to be friends, but there is a friend who sticks closer than a brother" (Prov. 18:24, TLB).

I know I depend on the type of friendship that sticks closer than a brother, not only with Jesus but also with very close brothers and sisters. These are the friends who accept you and encourage you to be more than you can see in yourself.

That's what Debbie was thinking about in the second verse of "Friends." She used the line right out of the letter of Colossians, which opens with Paul telling his friends:

> We give thanks to the God and Father of our Lord Jesus Christ, praying always for you, since we heard of your faith in Christ Jesus and of your love for all the saints; because of the hope which is laid up for you in heaven. (Col. 1:3–5, NKJV)

The main message of the song is that real friends are never parted. Real "friends are friends forever if the Lord's the Lord of them." And the chorus goes on to say, And a *friend will not say never 'cause the welcome will not end.* There aren't any "nevers" among friends except maybe, "I'll never give up on you, quit on you, or leave you in the lurch." Good friends are always there, and when they know each other in Christ, they know they will be friends eternally. There will be no separation.

If a friend disappoints you, goes off the deep end, does something stupid, or even repulsive, that friend is still your friend. You do not say, "I'll never trust you or like you again." You're always ready to forgive and start over with a friend.

The Secret of True Friendship

"How can I have friends?" I get asked that question a lot. I think a lot of kids get it mixed up with, "How can I be popular?" The idea is, "If I'm popular, everyone will like me and want to be my friend." All that gets you is friends that don't last. Friends don't pick friends because they're popular. That just says, "Hey, I want you for a friend because of what you can do for me. I want everyone to know I've got someone really important for a friend."

The Bible has a different idea. Proverbs 17:17 says, "A true friend is always loyal, and a brother is born to help in time of need" (TLB).

To have friends, be one. Don't wait for someone to pick you out and do everything that pleases you. Look around. There are dozens of people in your classes in school, at work, or on the team, who are looking for friends. They may not be the most popular kids, but that doesn't mean they won't make good friends. In fact, they usually make better, longer-lasting friends than the popular types.

To have friends, be a listener. What word do you think people use the most all day long? The telephone company did a study of this by listening to 500 telephone conversations. The word that was used 3,990 times was "I." Usually, when you are using the pronoun "I," you are referring to yourself and what you mainly are interested in and what you think.

To have friends, be unpossessive. In other words, don't hang on your friends as if you can't live without them. Have you ever had a friend who got upset if you wanted some time to yourself, or maybe some time with other people? This kind of friend literally tries to control you and to run your life. The normal reaction is to drop this person as quickly as possible. No one likes being smothered.

To have friends, be yourself. Don't try to be someone you're not in order to please people you think are cool, popular, or in with the right people. That's the trap I fell into in high school, and I paid a very heavy price.

I see a lot of kids who are intimidated. They want so badly to be accepted, and they know (or think they know) they're not being accepted. So how do they break that barrier? Usually they'll go along and do whatever the leaders of the in-crowd want.

I know now that a better plan is to have the guts to be who you are and nobody else. And what if you don't feel that strong and courageous? Ask God to give you courage. Pray that God will give you the right friends. I talk to a lot of kids who don't pray much. They tell me they just don't believe it works, and I tell them I know it does. If there is a need in your life, God will meet that need. God will answer that prayer— maybe not today or even next week, but He will answer it if you will hang in there and keep asking with faith and the desire to have what He wants in your life.

God can bring the right kind of friends. Make Jesus your best Friend. He'll take it from there!

chapter nine

Is Feeling Good, Good Enough?

L inda began her letter with:

> I hope that you will not find me disrespectful if
> I "talk" to you as if you were an old friend. . . .

She went on to share how she enjoyed one of our concerts, how her family had moved to a different part of the country and things had not worked out for her dad on his new job, how she struggled with adjusting to a new school and other problems.

And then she casually mentioned,

> Oh, yes. I met someone who is so nice . . . He is twenty (I'm sixteen) and a youth minister. My parents have previously told me no to going out with guys that much older. If you have any suggestions, I am open for them!

I get quite a few letters that ask me for advice, and they often focus on relationships. Is it safe for a sixteen-year-old to go out with a guy four years older? If teens do decide to date, what are the guidelines?

One obvious guideline is that they both have the same values and beliefs about God's gift of sex. If her twenty-year-old friend believes the Bible that he is teaching and modeling as a youth director in a church, he will want to treat Linda with care and respect. Then, if he can sell her parents, maybe he can date her with their approval.

Used Furniture

Whatever happens, Linda doesn't want anyone like the guy who talked with Josh McDowell during Easter week at Daytona Beach. After speaking to a big crowd of kids on the beach, Josh, a well-known writer and speaker for college students, was confronted by Dave. Dave wanted to know, "What's wrong with having meaningful sex if you don't want to hurt anybody and if you just want to enjoy yourself?"

It turned out that Dave claimed to have had intercourse with twenty-six women. Josh asked him one question: "Tell me . . . when you get married, do you want to marry a woman that's been one of the twenty-five meaningful relationships of another guy?" Of course Dave said no.

Dave's hypocrisy is pretty easy to spot. He doesn't see anything wrong with having "meaningful" relationships with woman after woman while hoping that he will marry a virgin. As Josh McDowell observes, "Most guys don't like used furniture, but they love to be in the antiquing business."[1]

Getting back to Linda's situation, she's asking the right questions before she gets into a pressure situation. We get many letters from girls who are being pressured to give up their most precious possession by guys who want them to "prove that you love me." We wrote "Old Enough to Know" as an answer to this kind of pressure:

> In the passion your heart is abused . . . He is pushing you, you have to choose . . . Oh, Rebecca, love is never . . . easy anymore . . . Oh, Rebecca, so afraid of . . . losing what is yours.

Chorus:

> Are you giving in to the pressure . . .
> Holding you again, now he tells you . . . what
> it takes to be in love . . . He believes you're
> old enough . . . but how you gonna feel tomor-
> row . . . when the day reveals . . . what you
> believed was for the sake of love . . . Don't
> you think you're old enough to know.

We Get Letters from Rebecca

Since the *Big Picture* album came out, we have gotten several letters from girls who know this song was written "just
for them." For example:

> I really like all the songs on your album, but one,
> "Old Enough to Know," is especially meaningful to me.
> My name is Rebecca and I am nineteen years old.
> Every word of that song applies to my life. Many
> times I am faced with those same temptations and
> pressures. I have been a Christian for many years,
> but still need support and encouragement from time
> to time. I really feel that God used you to write
> that song for me. Thank you.
>
> My name is Rebecca and I just went through the
> very experience your song talks about. My heart was

abused "in the passion" and I was hurt deeply for holding on to what is mine. I had been dating this guy for a year and then, boom, it was over. Needless to say, the Lord knew exactly what He was doing. I realized how Bobby had been the center of my life instead of my Savior. I am very thankful for the break-up now! . . . Your song describes me to a "T." No kidding, I am holding on to my romantic dream. I know God has someone whose love is patient and whose love would understand. I'm just trying to be patient and be filled with the Holy Spirit. I'm learning to fall in love with Jesus before I fall in love with any man.

A special letter from a youth director tells about a retreat he held for his youth group and one of the young girls in the group who heard "Old Enough to Know." This girl had been sexually active. The youth director writes:

No question what this lady's name was—Rebecca! Immediately she made the song hers and is also convinced God laid that song on your heart for her. Rebecca was so touched by your song that she wept all the next day and asked me to play that song for the entire youth group to let them know where she was and where the Lord brought her. That's courage. If only we could all be so transparent.

Guys Get Pressured, Too

These letters point out that how you use God's gift of sex is a decision that is in your hands and nobody else's. I think that goes for guys as well as girls—maybe more so. The typical stereotype is that girls are doing their best to protect their virginity while guys are doing their best to score, especially with virgins.

But this is misleading and untrue. A lot of guys want to be gentlemen, but they are being pressured also. The System squeezes them. If they haven't had a girl to bed or to a backseat by age sixteen, they just aren't real men! If they try to respect girls, somebody asks, "What's the matter. Are you gay?"

Recently there has been a lot of advertising and talk about using condoms for "safe sex." There may be a birth control or AIDS prevention clinic operating in your community or even in your school. What Christian teenagers and college students have to realize is that all this advertising and education isn't offering "safe sex." It is offering a way to have "safe sin."

But sin is never safe. There is a lot more to sex than thinking you know all about how the plumbing works and how to use the right equipment. What about the mental, emotional, and spiritual consequences? Often they are far greater.

Some women claim that having an abortion doesn't affect them. They say it was the "best thing they could have done." But what they don't tell people is that later on they wake up in the middle of the night sobbing uncontrollably after dreaming about what the baby might have been like. Abortion is not the answer.

Is God "Down on Sex"?

When God gave sex to men and women, He gave them a wonderful gift—and a tremendous responsibility. Is it any wonder, then, that the Bible tells us to handle sex with care? A lot of self-appointed experts who seldom open a Bible claim God is against sex. Nothing could be farther from the truth. What God is against is the stupid, selfish use of sex to gratify lust. Of course the Bible warns against stupid sex because God created sex for your good and enjoyment—to be done in the right place at the right time—within marriage with someone you love in a lifetime commitment.

When Paul wrote to the many churches he started, he often warned against fornication (sex before marriage) and adultery (betraying your marriage partner). Many of the new Christians in these churches had come out of pagan backgrounds where they had sex when and where they pleased with anyone who was willing to go along with them. (Does all this sound vaguely familiar?)

That's why Paul wrote to the church at Thessalonica and said: "[Be holy] . . . keep clear of all sexual sin [fornication]" (1 Thess. 4:3, TLB). Paul advised the Thessalonian Christians to learn how to control their bodies in a way that was holy and honorable instead of giving in to "passionate lust like the heathen, who do not know God" (1 Thess. 4:5, NIV).

Paul faced the problem of sexual immorality in almost every church he founded. He had to write to the Corinthians and tell them to discipline one of their members who was doing something that would shock even the heathen and pagans—sleeping with his father's wife. It's possible she was his stepmother, but that doesn't make it any less sick (see 1 Cor. 5:1–2).

Paul told the Ephesian Christians there should not be even a "hint of sexual immorality" among them because they were God's holy people (Eph. 5:3, NIV).

He told the Colossian Christians to "deaden the evil desires lurking within you; have nothing to do with sexual sin, impurity, lust and shameful desires" (Col. 3:5, TLB).

What If You "Really Love Each Other"?

There is that well-known argument: "But we love each other, and we know God understands." A lot of Christian couples use this excuse to have sex before marriage because they know they are going to get married anyway.

One basic reason God is against sex before marriage is that He wants marriage to really mean something. He also wants His Word to mean something. When two Christians decide they can have sex before making their vows, they are simply saying, "Sorry, Lord, Your standards are cramping our style. We know best, and it won't hurt to bend Your rules a little."

But fornication isn't "bending" God's rules, it's breaking them. Scripture plainly says, "Marriage should be honored by all, and the marriage bed kept pure, for God will judge the adulterer and all the sexually immoral" (Heb. 13:4, NIV).

It takes tremendous commitment, dedication, and courage for Christians to put these teachings into practice in a society that glorifies and idolizes stupid sex. Turn on the TV at just about any hour of the day or night and you can find a program or film that shows people committing fornication or adultery in all kinds of glamorous, exciting situations.

Experts disagree about what happens to your mind when you watch this kind of stuff week after week. Some say it doesn't really affect you, but others say it does. Who is right?

Well, think about it for a minute. What is a better way for The System to cook you in its own hot tub? What is a better way for The System to undermine the teachings from God's Word? When you watch adultery and fornication committed by beautiful, handsome, cool, and very likable people week after week, pretty soon you start thinking, *If this is the way life really is, it must be OK.* But it's not OK—for a lot of reasons.

We've already looked at the first reason to avoid fornication and adultery. God forbids both. It's His Word against Johnny's, or Sylvia's, or whoever is trying to talk you into "going all the way." And what about going "part way"? The Bible doesn't talk about "partial fornication" or "semi-adultery." In fact, Jesus taught that a man can commit adultery in his heart simply by lusting. It becomes obvious that we must protect our hearts at all cost. No matter how tough it is, we've got to stand firm.

Five More Reasons to Handle Sex with Care

Why does God's Word put "handle with care" signs all around this area of life called sex? Dr. Kevin Leman, psychologist who wrote *Smart Kids, Stupid Choices*[2] and who speaks all over the country, often shares the following points with teenagers or college students on why it's best to save sex for marriage only.

1. Sex precludes or prevents intimacy. A lot of people think the physical act of sex is "being intimate," but it is only a very small part of the picture. A lot of guys use the line that "sex will help us to really get to know each another." Ask countless numbers of girls who have given in to guys, and they'll tell you that their "boyfriends" never really wanted to get to know them as persons. They didn't want real intimacy. All they wanted was the sex.

2. Sex before marriage can ruin a good relationship. Developing a relationship with someone of the opposite sex is much like weaving a fine piece of cloth. When sex comes into the relationship before its proper place and time, it can rip and tear that cloth. Yes, a lot of couples do have sex before marriage and then get married anyway. Sometimes it works out, but many times it doesn't. Dr. Leman counsels many women who are having marital troubles that can be traced right back to putting too much emphasis on the physical before marriage.

3. Sex outside marriage with someone who is "sure he / she loves you" can end up in a case of herpes or something more deadly like AIDS. In one of his recent books, Dr. Leman writes: "It is ironic that society seems to have suddenly discovered condoms because of the AIDS scare. 'At least wear a condom and don't risk dying' is the message in the new ads appearing in print or in TV screens. All this sudden concern about condoms is not caused by fear of pregnancy—it is fear of dying a slow, horrible death. Lost in the panicky din about AIDS is a real point: Sex *is not something to be done recreationally or as a way to get to know each other.*"[3]

4. Having sex can trap you into an unwanted marriage. Dr. Leman counsels many married couples who were pregnant at the altar. They went ahead and got married, but there was a resentment and a reluctance that finally surfaced years later in marital problems. Sex before marriage can plant seeds of distrust that can sprout in strange ways ten or fifteen years after the wedding.

5. Sex before marriage can lead to being tempted, urged, or forced to have an abortion. Is an unborn baby a person? Read

Psalm 139:13–14. Does David sound as if he is writing about a thing? "For you created my inmost being; you knit me together in my mother's womb. I praise you because I am fearfully and wonderfully made; your works are wonderful, I know that full well" (NIV).

Any couple that uses the abortion solution to their "problem" faces the lifelong guilt of knowing they took another human life. Notice I said "couple," not just woman. When an unmarried woman has an abortion, the father of the baby must take responsibility also.

Love Is a Decision, Not a Feeling

Dr. Leman stresses that love is not a feeling, it is a decision. One of the favorite expressions you hear today is "Follow your feelings." That sounds attractive and romantic, but what if everyone lived that way? What if everyone just followed his or her feelings on the freeway driving to work some morning? What if you just decided to follow your feelings when you were "too tired to study" before finals? What if we all just followed our feelings every time we got angry with each other?

Dr. Leman writes, "Love is not a feeling. Love is not 'the tinglies.' Love is a decision that we must make every day to put someone else first in life. In a marriage, that someone else is your spouse. Love is a cognitive, willful act. Feelings have very little to do with it, particularly around three o'clock in the morning when the baby needs changing or somebody has 'lost it' before getting to the bathroom to throw up."[4]

To illustrate the difference between deciding to love someone and just "following your feelings," I worked out the following chart that compares love and lust. Love comes out of a decision. Lust comes out of feelings.

LOVE:	LUST:
According to God's Word (1 Cor. 13:4–7)	According to the values of The System—"let's follow our feelings"
Is patient	Is always in a hurry
Is kind	Is smooth and persuasive
Does not envy	Wants everyone to envy its "accomplishments"— especially in bed
Does not boast	Enjoys "telling the guys how I scored"
Is not proud	Is driven by pride
Is not rude	Doesn't respect feelings or anyone else
Is not self-seeking	Is always seeking to please *only* itself
Is not easily angered	Gets angry if you "don't love me enough to prove it"
Keeps no record of wrongs	Keeps score after score after score
Does not delight in evil but rejoices in the truth	Loves evil and willingly lies to get what it wants
Always protects	Always harms
Always trusts	Tries to "do it to others before they do it to me"
Always hopes	Has no real hope
Always perseveres	Also perseveres—to do evil

I get a lot of letters from kids who are locked into their youth group and are involved in the whole church scene. They have the right motives and a godly desire to be pure and holy. But the pressure to be sexually active is unbelievable. I won't give you any "cold shower" advice, but I will suggest that you stop to pray whenever you face a decision between love and lust, between following your feelings and following Christ.

The most important thing to remember—*before* you get yourself into a situation where feelings have taken over completely and your brain is in neutral—is to *STOP TO THINK*. And then turn and walk away. You've got to walk away from it because there's no way you can get close to the fire and not get burned. The Bible is right: You reap what you sow (see Gal. 6:7). As the second verse of "Old Enough to Know" says:

You're a breed of few and far between . . . holding on to your romantic dream . . . Oh, Rebecca, love is patient . . . love would understand . . . Oh, Rebecca, your decision . . . is your only chance . . . Oh, Rebecca, don't confuse what love is . . . with what some say love should be . . .

Goin' Nowhere Fast

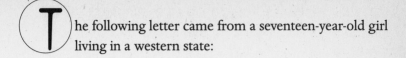

The following letter came from a seventeen-year-old girl living in a western state:

> Dear Michael, I have grown up in a Christian home. My parents are great. I have wonderful Christian friends. I am part of an active youth ministry with a great youth minister. No one has ever offered me drugs, I'm not going to commit suicide, I'm not even dating.
>
> It seemed like I couldn't relate to the millions of teenagers out there—and that a lot of the Christian music out there didn't relate to me. I guess that must make me look like some sort of "goody two-shoes," but that doesn't mean I don't struggle with other things. The girls who date are faced with the pressure of holding on to their virginity. Those of us who haven't dated—it doesn't do a great deal for your self-image to be seventeen and spend your weekends with a trig or chemistry book. You know?

I appreciate this letter because the teenager who wrote it was honest enough to admit that even when you have a lot of good things going for you, life can get discouraging.

Why "Emily" Was Written

I had just worked out a new tune that I wanted to make a song of encouragement for a teenager—anyone who just feels life is going nowhere fast. Wayne Kirkpatrick, who wrote most of the lyrics for *The Big Picture* album, took the melody and worked up a special message for his younger brother who was still in high school and who was really struggling with his grades, his job, his social life—you name it.

> Caught in an endless time . . . waiting for a sign . . . to show you where to go . . . Lost in a silent stare . . . looking anywhere . . . for answers you don't know . . .
>
> On the wire, balancing your dreams . . . hoping ends will meet their means . . . But you feel alone . . . uninspired. Well does it help you to . . . know that I believe in you . . . You're an angel waiting for wings, Emily . . .

Wayne's brother was definitely caught in that "endless time" waiting for some kind of a sign, some kind of encouragement. Wayne wanted him to know that the endless time would end, that a lot of people believed in him and someday he would spread his wings.

High school, especially, is the "will you ever?" time of life. Will you ever get dates, or are you doomed to spending Saturday nights with a chemistry book? Will you ever get all the credits you need to graduate? Will you ever be able to afford that car you want? Will you ever make the team or get to start a game or get a driver's license? Or whatever. You're on that high wire, balancing your dreams, feeling alone and uninspired.

I know the feeling. I had it in high school and during those college years at Marshall University. I was caught, trapped, wondering what to do and where to go. The weeks seemed like months, and every month was a year.

My Family Pulled Me Through

What helped pull me through was knowing my parents believed in me. They never hassled or nagged. They encouraged—and prayed—and prayed some more. My mom and dad were a great combination of solid faith and love. They believed the Bible, and they practiced it.

So did my grandmother. "Nanny" saw that I had musical potential and started giving me piano lessons when I was only six or seven. Naturally, I didn't like to practice. Because I was able to play by ear, I'd ask Nanny to play my practice pieces for me, and then, of course, I could play them back with no trouble. But after a while she caught on to that and wouldn't do it for me anymore. She forced me to try to read the notes and practice correctly.

Nanny disciplined me, but she was never mean. Actually, she was the sweetest lady—sometimes even sweeter than my own mom, as grandparents can be when they spoil you a little.

In the fall of 1982, we were winding up a tour, and Nanny came up to Louisville, Kentucky, on a Thursday night to hear me sing and play. She had heart problems and couldn't get around very well, but she came anyway and had a terrific time. She heard me on Thursday night and went back home. By Friday night Nanny was gone. She went to sleep and woke up in the presence of Jesus. And there's still not a day that goes by that I don't miss Nanny and the influence she had on my life.

If Your Family Isn't Supportive

With all that support I had from my family, I still had those times of discouragement, feeling depressed and down. I know that for many kids who write to me, it's a lot tougher because their families are not supportive at all. Their letters describe how it feels:

Sharon:

> All of a sudden one night we got in a huge fight. . . . Then my parents got really mad at each other and my dad left . . . So then my mom starts crying and blaming me for everything that had just happened, which left me feeling awful, so I started thinking, "They've told me before that I should have been born in another family . . ." So then I decided, if they hate me so much, why don't they just send me away or just shoot me?! So, by then I was totally irrational and (after a lot of thought) I decided that life was not for me. God had played some kind of awful mean joke on my parents by even having me exist . . .

Bobbie:

> My parents are in the process of divorcing and I've been "running" since December. Dad's an alcoholic. . . . A lot has happened. I just hurt so much and I know I've been putting barbed wire around my heart.

Rachael:

> I'm sure glad you made that little comment at the concert that we're all in this together—we all have problems. 'Cause sometimes I get real depressed because my parents don't really understand me and we don't really get along that well! I know that often God is the closest when you feel really depressed and lonely or when you're really hurting. I get depressed when my parents say I don't try and when I try to tell them, it's a waste of air. It seems that my mom often puts me down. Sometimes I feel like saying to her, "Can't you accept me the way I am?"

You Have a Secret Weapon

What's the answer to feeling discouraged and depressed? Part of it is in the second verse of "Emily":

> You, going through this stage . . . it's a restless age . . . young and insecure . . . still, there are doubts to fade . . . moments to be made . . . and one of them is yours . . .

It may not always be good news to hear that you're going through a stage, but it's true. Everybody—at every age—is always going through some stage of development in his or her life. The great thing about being young, though, is that you have so much potential. According to the dictionary, "potential" is something that is possible, but it hasn't happened yet. *Potential* is the "built-in ability or capacity for growing, developing, or becoming something special."

"Emily" has a message that is very similar to "You're Alright." When we sing "Emily" at a concert, I think of all the things kids are dealing with—peer pressure, possible trouble at home, depression, even thoughts of suicide, drugs, alcohol, you name it. What I'm trying to say with this tune is, "I really believe in you. Each and every one of you has tremendous potential." I want everybody who hears me sing to know that "I believe in you."

I'm convinced that each of us has phenomenal individual gifts that can be perfected. You may not even have a good idea of what those gifts are, but they are there, lying deep within you, waiting to be discovered. There are moments ahead to be made, and one of them is yours! "Emily" is a real encouragement song for a real tough time, especially for kids who are thirteen, fourteen, and fifteen years old. That's the stage when you're too old to be treated like a child, but too young for so many things—too young to drive, too young to be trusted with certain responsibilities, maybe too young to date, etc.

It's tough to see much potential in your life when your self-esteem is gone and your self-image is one-dimensional—totally flat. Much of our self-image is wrapped up in how well we think we are doing. Remember the three-legged stool of self-esteem mentioned in chapter one? One of those legs was "feeling capable and confident." It's important to gain skills and competence, but be careful. If you base your total feelings of self-worth on how well you perform, you can always be chasing the carrot that is constantly dangling out there just beyond your reach.

Practical or Neurotic Perfectionist?

A lot of people are perfectionists; they fall for the idea that they have to do everything perfectly in order to be accepted. It's great to strive for excellence and to do the best you can, but stop to think about your motives. Are you a practical or a neurotic perfectionist?

The neurotic perfectionists are never happy with what they do. They always think it can be a little better, a little smoother or faster—or whatever it is supposed to take to be "perfect." Neurotic perfectionists are never finished; they're always unsatisfied, and they're never sure people like them for who they are instead of simply how well they perform.

Practical perfectionists, however, give things their best shot, know when to quit, and are able to be satisfied with knowing that they gave it their best shot.

Obviously, practical perfectionists are far more likely to have good self-esteem. Of course, you may be saying that you're no perfectionist at all. In fact, your parents and teachers get on your case because you don't try hard enough. This could be a reverse form of perfectionism. You aren't trying hard because you don't think you can do well enough. You prefer hiding in your shell, and that doesn't do anything for your self-esteem either.

It always comes back to balance. In his letter to the Ephesian church, Paul explains that Christians aren't saved because of perfect performances or a lot of good works (see Eph. 2:8–9). Their salvation comes from God as a free gift because of His grace (His love and favor that we could never earn ourselves). Neurotic perfectionists try to earn their own salvation by being good enough and living the "perfect life." That's why they are doomed to be neurotic and unhappy.

Practical perfectionists accept God's free gift of salvation by faith, but then they go on to live the best lives they can because they realize:

> It is God Himself who has made us what we are and given us new lives from Christ Jesus; and long ages ago He planned that we should spend these lives in helping others. (Eph. 2:10, TLB)

To sum it up, don't perform to earn the acceptance of God or anyone else; give things your best shot because you know who you are in Christ. People with good self-esteem make an honest effort to do the best they can. If they gain attention, that's great. If they happen to be overlooked, it's no big deal; their self-esteem is still in one piece.

Will I Ever Make Anything of Myself?

High schoolers are at such an awkward age. You've got so many things you want to do, but you're insecure about what you're able to do. You just keep wondering if you're going to make anything of yourself. It really helps to know that there is someone out there who is behind you—who believes in you.

Like me, Wayne Kirkpatrick was also fortunate enough to have a family who gave him tremedous love and support. In writing the lyrics to "Emily" he tried to return the favor to his younger brother. Younger kids are often intimidated by their older brothers and sisters who may have already gotten on with their accomplishments in life. The youngest one may feel that he's been left behind and that he has to walk in the shadows of the people ahead of him. He really needs to hear that someone believes in him.

It can be devastating to feel intimidated—afraid and fearful. I can recall how our football team at C-K High School suffered one of its few losses by being intimidated. During my senior year, we only lost one game. We went out into the country to play this team, which was only having an average year. But the word was out. "We're going to beat you. We're going to wipe you guys out!"

For some reason that no one on our team could explain, we didn't have our usual energy. We were actually scared we'd be beaten. We were intimidated. We didn't take this team too lightly. We took them too seriously and lost twelve to seven.

We went on to win the state championship, and Wayne High School went on to have a so-so season, but they didn't care. They had beaten the state champs, and that made their season.

Our loss to a team that had no business beating us is a good example of the power of self-image. There is a saying: "What I see is who I'll be." If you see yourself as strong, capable, and going places, that's what you'll be. If you see yourself as going nowhere fast, a victim, somebody caught on an endless treadmill and serving endless time before getting out of school, that's what you'll be.

We Are Unworthy, but Not Worthless

Who are you? You are a person, made in God's image (see Gen. 1:26, 28). If Christ is your Savior, you are redeemed by His sacrificial death for your sins (see Rom. 3:23–26; Col. 1:13, 15).

It's true we are unworthy of what God has done for us by sending His Son to die on the cross for our sins. It's true there is nothing we can do to deserve God's grace. If God treated us justly, we would be doomed to die in our sins, but God's love satisfied His justice by putting Christ in our place. We may be unworthy, but we aren't worthless. Scripture says we have been made a little lower than angels and God has crowned us with glory and honor (see Ps. 8:4–5). Who are you? You are God's beloved child, and He knows all about your endless time and feelings of goin' nowhere fast.

I got a great letter from Cheryl, who shared how she coped during her "Emily" time. She had been feeling down and depressed and had developed an ulcer.

She found herself in her room crying all the time. She lost several friends, including one guy who dropped out of school to lose himself in drugs. She had given up a lot of activities like piano and voice lessons, and now her self-esteem was at the all-time low.

Cheryl felt useless. Finally she wound up in the hospital with anemia, and they sent in a psychologist to talk with her. Talking with the psychologist really didn't change anything, but after getting out of the hospital Cheryl told herself something had to happen soon. This depression was totally ruining her life.

That summer she went camping with her family near a gorgeous lake. Right around sunset one day she decided to go for a walk and be alone. And Cheryl's letter goes on to say:

> I walked about a half mile to the beach. There wasn't anyone around so I was totally alone. The sun was setting so it was the most beautiful scene I had ever seen. I started talking to God, and I started crying, but it wasn't the same kind of

crying I was used to. I had a special feeling in me, I don't know, I can't really explain it. But it felt like I had lost that awful depressed feeling I had for so long and it was being replaced by something new. I felt so good, and I rededicated my life to Christ because I wanted to start over and needed Him to take away all the pain I had. And He did. And since then I think I've been really happy nearly every day.

Is there anything in Cheryl's story that you can use to cope with discouragement and depression? I think so. You don't necessarily have to be by a lake watching a beautiful sunset. You can do what she did just about anywhere. Cheryl never gave up staying in touch with God. She kept praying and trusting and reaching out to Him, and He answered.

The same thing can happen for you or anyone else who is willing to have just a little bit of faith and let God take it from there. The endless time of waiting will open up into what seems like endless opportunities. Your doubts will fade, and you will spread your wings.

Be patient. As the Bible says, some day you will have strength to fly like an eagle (see Isa. 40:31). Your moments are out there, and you have the potential to make them unforgettable!

chapter eleven

What's Life for, Anyway?

Back in chapter three, I mentioned my friend Dan, a fantastic artist who could have been one of the greats. It didn't happen because Dan died too young.

Dan was living in Nashville at the time, and I was staying in close touch with him to try to help him with his many problems, the worst of which was heavy drinking. When he drank, he became a different person. He would call me up and want to talk, so I'd drive across town and we'd spend hours together. I'd try to encourage him and remind him of his roots, which were in Christ and the church. Dan had a lot of biblical knowledge, but he didn't know how to turn the power of God loose in his life.

In January 1981, Dan was living in a "halfway house" in Nashville. His wife and children had separated from him temporarily and were living in Kenova. I kept encouraging Dan and finally was able to put him in touch with a publishing house who liked his artwork.

Things were looking up. Despite his own troubles with alcohol, Dan was trying to help some of the other guys in the halfway house. He was even working on getting one man to attend AA meetings, but he really needed AA more himself. When something would happen and life would close in, it would set Dan off.

The day after I got him the contact with a publisher, Dan called, drunk. He told me he had filed for divorce and that really ticked me off. "What did you do that for? I can't believe you did that," I told him. We argued and he finally hung up on me. And for once I didn't go over to see him and talk with him.

I learned later that Dan went out and used some food stamps to get a big basket of groceries. He came back to the halfway house and fed a lot of hungry guys who'd come in off the streets of Nashville for shelter. Then Dan went back to his room, took off his bathrobe belt, put it around his neck, and hanged himself.

Letters from Kids Poured In

Dan's death devastated all of us. I was a basket case of mixed emotions—feeling guilty, depressed, and also angry with my friend who had done this terrible, senseless thing. He had wasted himself and his incredible God-given talent as an artist. He had left terrible pain behind in his wife, children, and parents.

Could I have helped Dan more? Should I have gone over to see him after our argument on the phone? The questions haunted my mind, and the guilt flooded in, but I finally came to terms with it. I had tried to help Dan, but I realized I couldn't take care of him. I couldn't replace God.

While I didn't forget Dan—and never will—I thought I would probably never come that close to someone suicidal again. But I was wrong. As soon as the *Michael W. Smith Project* album came out, the letters started coming in. Many of the kids wrote about low self-esteem, problems with parents, problems with friends and peer pressure, being depressed, in pain—and ready just to end it now.

More than six thousand teenagers each year decide that there is no way out and commit suicide. It was out of this kind of need that Wayne Kirkpatrick and I wrote "The Last Letter." We weren't sure what we had when we were finished. Is suicide a suitable subject for a song? Secular rock stars have put out stuff that urges people to try it, and some of them do.

John Tried "Killing Himself to Live"

At the age of sixteen, John Tanner put a shotgun to his chin, told God he was coming home, and pulled the trigger. The blast took off his face but did not kill him. Over the next ten years it took twenty operations to reconstruct what he blew away in a second.

Why did John try to kill himself? John admits:

> I just lost my sense of worth through listening to a lot of acid rock and smoking pot. . . . I really didn't appreciate anything anymore. I started looking at the negative side of things. It just built up inside of me.

John had several favorite rock groups including Black Sabbath. He remembers especially their songs "Killing Yourself to Live," "After Forever," and "Into the Void," which he listened to a great deal before he shot himself.

> I was getting more depressed, especially after I decided to do it. I wasn't thinking realistically. Then the day I shot myself, I skipped out of school and stayed in my room and listened to albums all day. . . . I think from being real dedicated to Black Sabbath—because they are really depressing—that I got from them a real deep depression, and I'd say that's where the suicide stems from.[1]

To put out one song like "The Last Letter" almost seems like trying to plug a ten-foot hole in the dike with one finger. But we had to try to send a message of hope to kids who have become so depressed or angry that suicide seems like the only solution.

The first verse of "The Last Letter" sets the stage to let depressed teenagers know that saying "good-bye" through suicide is no solution at all:

> Sitting alone up in your empty room . . . in the stillness of the night . . . where all the many dreams that used to carry you . . . are no longer in sight . . . You put your feelings down in black and white . . . a sad, disturbing reply . . . that you don't really want to face another night . . . So you're saying good-bye . . . but do you know that you're saying good-bye . . . to a lifetime . . .

Wayne and I weren't experts on suicide. But we tried to catch that feeling of hopelessness, of seeing no future ahead—the shattering of dreams, and just not wanting to face another night or day. Suicidal people just want out. They want to say "good-bye" to their troubles. It isn't that they necessarily want to die, but they can't handle life as it is. We wanted to let them know they *can* handle it—if they ask for help. The chorus tells how:

> Well, I've got to tell you there's another way . . . to be free—to be complete . . . but, you've

got to make it through another day . . . and
deny your own defeat (don't give in) . . . And
I'm here to tell you there's another way . . .
to consume a hungry heart . . . All the love you
need is just a prayer away . . . Let it in to
where you are . . .

They Heard "The Last Letter" Just in Time

Since *The Big Picture* album came out, many other letters
have come in to tell us "The Last Letter" has helped deeply
depressed kids realize there is hope.

Heather wrote to say:

> Two weeks ago I was ready to throw the towel
> in . . . Last Saturday I was really confused. I went
> shopping and I ended up getting your last album. I
> came home and was ready to give up. I listened to
> "The Last Letter" for the first time. The chorus
> of the song made me realize that God is there,
> if I can see Him or not. Thank you A LOT!

Debbie, a fourteen-year-old living in the Southwest, wrote
to say that her family had been moving from state to state and
it was tough because every time she started to make new
friends she had to leave them. Her letter continued:

> About two months ago I heard your song "The
> Last Letter." At first I didn't really pay much

attention, but after I wanted to commit suicide, I understood. Everything was going wrong. School, friends, and boyfriend . . . he thought it would be better to break up. He says we're two different people.

After that I went to my room. I was very upset. I didn't want to live without him.

There was a bottle of Pine Sol cleaner in my bathroom. I went in and kneeled down. I was going to do it. Everyone and everything I've ever loved has been taken away from me, so why should I go on living? Just to get hurt? No, I hated myself so much I opened the bottle, and I said, "Satan, you've won."

During this I hadn't realized the radio was on and your song was playing. "Jesus is only a prayer away." How true! I dropped the bottle and fell on my face. I begged forgiveness and prayed. About three days later my boyfriend called back and he was sorry and he wanted to give it a shot again. Ever since that he's really opened to Jesus and things are looking up. There is power in prayer. I don't know how to thank you enough . . .

When Wayne and I hear from a Heather or a Debbie, we're thankful "The Last Letter" is communicating what we tried to say:

> Don't give up . . . don't quit on life and
> yourself . . . there is hope . . . there is a
> better way to be free and complete.

They Lost Hope

In March 1987, the nation was shocked by the deaths of
four teenagers—two boys and two girls—who died together
in the same car left running in a closed garage. Three of them
were school dropouts, one had been suspended and was talking about not going back. They all were on the outs with their
families, which had histories of divorce, violence, or crisis.

Newsweek magazine said, "They weren't criminals, just
troubled losers hanging aimlessly, drinking too much and
doing a little dope, 'going nowhere fast.'"[2]

Suicide was their final statement of desperation and
despair. In this case they all left notes, but whether suicidal
people leave notes or not, their statement is always there: "I
couldn't take it anymore. I don't see any point in going on
with this."

If you wanted to describe a suicidal person with one word,
a lot of people would pick "depressed." To be depressed literally means "to be flattened." To start thinking about suicide
means that you are beginning to lose hope. When you commit
suicide, you have decided all hope is gone. Life is totally flat.

Does Being a Christian Help?

Researchers have discovered that people with religious, and
particularly Christian, values are less apt to commit suicide.

But being a Christian is no guarantee you won't get depressed enough to think about it.

Many of the kids who write and mention suicide or at least thoughts of suicide are Christians. Others want God in their lives, but it doesn't "seem to be working." For example, Pam came to one of our concerts and wrote back later:

> When I came to your concert, I never expected you to touch my life with your ministry . . . [but] I couldn't help but cry during "Emily" and "Friends." I wanted so much to come back and talk to you afterwards, but it just didn't work out. So, ever since then, all I can do is stare at the words of your song. Every one of your songs fits my life. I'm at the lowest point, and I really don't know who to turn to. I've tried God, but He makes me more confused.
>
> All I really want is a friend who understands and can help me without judging me. This is "my last letter," the last time I'm trying to trust someone. You said you've been through "it" so maybe you will understand me. More than anything, I want to fulfill my dream. Can you help me fulfill my last wish before I'm through? Before I leave, I want to know that someone important cares about someone as small as me.

What could I say to Pam? I contacted her and tried to encourage her not to give up on God. I also shared that it's one thing to "try God," it's another to turn your life over to Jesus Christ. Only He can solve the feelings of alienation and loneliness that bring people to the brink of suicide. As the second verse of "The Last Letter" says:

You've made it to the edge of seventeen . . . thinking how you've reached the end of the line . . . But there is so much of life that you have never seen . . . now you won't have the time . . . You say that you don't hear the music play . . . so you're ready to give up the dance . . . Now that nothing really matters anyway . . . oh, you give up your chance . . . But do you know that you give up your chance . . . at a lifetime . . .

I am not a psychologist or a counselor with a suicide counseling clinic. But it's my prayer that "The Last Letter" will help some people change their minds and give themselves a chance.

If You Can't Trust God, Then What?

There are times when things just don't seem to be going right and times when you wonder if God's even listening. You look at life and see all the suffering and the pain. Life seems full of frustration.

There is a great verse in the letter from James that says, "Is your life full of difficulties and temptations? Then be happy, for when the way is rough, your patience has a chance to grow. So let it grow, and don't try to squirm out of your problems. For when your patience is finally in full bloom, then you will be ready for anything, strong in character, full and complete" (James 1:2–4, TLB).

Counselors will tell you that suicidal people feel ambivalent. Part of them wants to die, but part of them still wants to live. But the dreams that carried them have disappeared, and they don't want to face another night. Overwhelmed with the problems of the moment, they think they're willing to throw away a lifetime. As one suicide counselor bluntly tells kids, "Suicide is a permanent solution to a temporary problem. It's like cutting off your leg because your little toe hurts."[3]

In "The Last Letter," we aren't discounting teenage problems or judging anyone for having terrible feelings of depression and hopelessness. We just want to communicate that there is a way out. Better days will come. Whatever you're going through will pass. The chorus says:

> I'm here to tell you there's another way . . . to consume a hungry heart . . . Jesus is waiting just a prayer away . . . let Him in to where you are.

I am not trying to make depression, feelings of hopelessness and thoughts of suicide sound simplistic and, that all you have to do is "pray about it." God provides all kinds of resources, including doctors, psychologists, counselors, etc. For example, some depressed people have been greatly helped by carefully administered prescription drugs that help balance certain chemicals in the brain.

We should use all of the resources God has put at our disposal, but we should never forget to use prayer—the greatest resource of all. Through prayer *all* things are possible!

God Will Get You through It

Prayer is not some kind of magic wand that you can wave and everything will be all right again. But prayer is a way of talking with God, sharing your heart and letting Him know about the circumstances. God may not change the circumstances or get you out of them, but He will always get you through them.

Getting depressed enough to think about suicide doesn't happen in a moment, or even overnight. You can usually trace it back to continued feelings of anger, fear, anxiety, and worry. Recently I heard about the research study on fear that was done at the University of Michigan. It showed that 60 percent of our fears are unwarranted, and 20 percent have already become past events and are completely out of our control anyway. That leaves 20 percent, and of those fears only 4 or 5 percent are real and justifiable.

When you look at the 4 or 5 percent of "real" fears, at least half of them are things we can't do anything about. That means that only 2 or 2.5 percent of our fears are really worth thinking about at all, and we can handle them easily—if we stop playing victim and start dealing with our cares and worries in a positive way.[4]

Two passages that help me deal with my cares and fears are Philippians 4:6–7 and 1 Peter 5:7. Peter tells us that in His good time God will lift us up, and we should "let him have all your worries and cares, for he is always thinking about you and watching everything that concerns you" (1 Pet. 5:7, TLB).

You may be thinking that's easy for Peter to say because he didn't have your problems. No, he had far worse ones, and he was writing his letter to Christians who had been scattered in every direction by persecution of the first-century church.

But Peter knew that the only answer is to turn your troubles over to God. He'd heard Jesus teach in the Sermon on the Mount, "I tell you, do not worry about your life, what you will eat or drink; or about your body, what you will wear. Is not life more important than food and the body more important than clothes?" (Matt. 6:25, NIV).

And Peter could have been standing nearby when Jesus and His disciples visited Mary and Martha, and Martha got all upset because she had to do all the serving. When Martha complained that Mary wasn't doing any work, Jesus said, "Martha, Martha, . . . you are worried and upset about many things, but only one thing is needed. Mary has chosen what is better, and it will not be taken away from her" (Luke 10:41–42, NIV).

Pray First

Too often we fail to pray until things "get bad enough." Listen to Christians talk about their problems, and you will often hear something like, "Wow, this is serious—we had better pray." Prayer isn't the *last* thing you should do; it's the *first*. It isn't an emergency chute; it's what you should use so you won't have to bail out!

Two of the greatest verses on prayer in the Bible are Philippians 4:6–7: "Do not be anxious about anything, but in everything, by prayer and petition, with thanksgiving, present your requests to God. And the peace of God, which transcends all understanding, will guard your hearts and your minds in Christ Jesus" (NIV).

Paul knew what it was to be under pressure, to take all kinds of hard blows and persecution. Paul knew what it was to worry. In 2 Corinthians 4:8–9 he admitted, "We are hard pressed on every side, but not crushed; perplexed, but not in despair; persecuted, but not abandoned; struck down, but not destroyed" (NIV). Paul knew what it meant to be on the ropes and even down on the canvas, but he was never out. He never let worry eat him up. He never let problems drive him to despair and depression. And how did he do it? With prayer.

He says, "Pray about everything with thanksgiving." It's typical to pray only about certain things. We save prayer for the "really big things" that matter. Paul says, "In everything let your requests be made known to God."

And when you take *everything* to God in prayer, an awesome thing happens. You experience a peace that is beyond any human understanding. Christ literally guards your heart and mind the way soldiers guard a fortress. When Paul wrote these words, he was chained to a Roman guard, whose responsibility was not to let Paul escape or be harmed by the enemies, like some fanatical Jews who hated him and wanted him dead. Paul used his prison situation to paint a picture of how to protect yourself from the bad stuff that brings self-pity, depression, and despair.

What's life for, anyway? It's for living, not dying. God's love, help, joy—and peace—are only a prayer away.

chapter twelve

You're Never All Alone

How long do you think you could take being *totally alone?* A scientist in England named Smith (no relation) decided to answer the question by building an experimental, soundproof room 9´x 9´ x 7 1/2´ and suspending it with nylon ropes from the top of a huge building. Volunteers went into the room to see how long they could last in it alone. They had to wear padded fur gloves and heavy woolen socks to reduce any sensations of touch. They also wore translucent goggles to cut down vision.

Dr. Smith recorded the volunteers through a one-way screen; he could see in, but they could not see out. Everything, including eating meals, had to be done inside the boxlike isolation room suspended high above the ground in midair.

Dr. Smith observed that after an hour or so, most volunteers lost concentration. Next they suffered anxiety and feelings of panic. Most of them lasted in the room less than five hours overall.[1]

How long could you or I last in the isolation box? That's hard to say. A better question: How long can we last when life seems just about as lonely as being in that box? Friends leave or turn on you. Parents seem to ride your back. It feels as if the whole crowd is against you. From all the mail I get, it appears there are just about as many ways to be lonely as there are people.

Sheila's Special Love for Jesus

For example, Michelle lost her best friend and wrote to tell me:

> Through my younger teenage years I was a kid who had a hard nose and a rebellious heart toward

my parents, authority, or the word no! All through those years I had a girlfriend Sheila who stuck close to me through thick and thin. The thing that made her so special was her deep love for Jesus . . . Her favorite song was "Friends." She played it over and over, saying, "It's a promise made by man from God." . . . Sheila died in a car accident, and I have to admit I hated the world because of it . . . I have never had to deal with hurt that strong.

Another letter came from Judy, who feels lonely everywhere she turns:

School really has its ups and downs. It gets really frustrating. I guess it only depends on how you handle the downs. My mother is telling me I'm a worthless person. I don't know what to say to her now. How do you respond to something like that?

Terri's letter shared her horror of being raped and went on to say:

About six months later I went through a severe depression. I attempted suicide twice because life just wasn't worth living. "The Last Letter" tells how I felt.

Everyone Has the "Lonelies"

Loneliness, isolation, emptiness—everybody has those feelings at times. There are all kinds of ways to be lonely. You don't need an isolation box or a cell in solitary confinement. You can be lonely in a crowd at a football game or at a concert. Believe me, it can be lonely up there on stage, too!

It can be really lonely in a high school or college classroom when you don't feel part of the total scene, when you feel like an outsider. That's why we wrote, "I Know," which begins by describing the feeling you can get when peer pressure comes down on you like a collapsing building:

> Everybody's talking in the home room . . .
> Plans are being made for after school . . .
> Should you tell them how you're really feeling
> . . . or go along and play it cool . . . Well,
> I know—I know how you feel . . .
> Everybody's talking 'bout a good time . . .
> Something tells you something isn't right . . .
> but when you're lonely and the pressure's on you
> . . . it's really hard to stand and fight . . .
> Well, I know—I know how it feels . . . Torn
> between the mind of the crowd . . . and the matters of the heart . . . I know—I know how you feel . . .

I know plenty about that scene—not wanting to be left out but knowing something's not quite right with what your friends plan to do. I know how it feels when a good friend dies, and I definitely know what it's like to feel miserable and depressed, absolutely fed up with the way life is going.

I can't identify with all the lonely people, but there is Someone who can. That's why the chorus of "I Know" says this:

```
There's a light that holds you in the darkness
. . . There's a candle burning in the wind . . .
and if you can lean upon the Father . . . you
can find the strength within . . . I know that
you can . . .
```

Crutch or Counselor?

The primary purpose of this book and every song that we do is to help you learn to lean upon the Father. Atheists and agnostics like to say Christians need God for a "crutch." The answer to that is, "Yes, you're right, and who isn't limping?" But when Christ is your Savior, God is more than your crutch; He's also your Guide, Counselor, and Friend, and He's always with you.

There are lots of great passages in Scripture that tell us God will never leave us alone. The writer of the letter to the Hebrews reminded them of God's promises to His people in the Old Testament. In Hebrews, chapter 13, verses 5–6 (NIV), he quotes: "Never will I leave you; never will I forsake you" (see Deut. 31:6). "I will not be afraid . . . The LORD is my helper" (see Ps. 118:6–7).

The same promises are for us today and so is the promise Jesus made to His disciples before He ascended into heaven:

"And surely I will be with you always, to the very end of the age" (Matt. 28:20, NIV).

Where to Go When You're Lonely

Next to Psalm 139, perhaps my favorite Scripture is Romans 8:28–39. Whenever I'm feeling lonely, isolated, and out of it, I go to this passage and remember that I can know ". . . in all *things* God works for the good of those who love him, who have been called according to his purpose" (Rom. 8:28, NIV).

A lot of people are familiar with the King James Version of Romans 8:28, which says: "We know that all things work together for good to them that love God . . ." Quoting that version to someone in deep pain or sorrow can sound cold and even almost meaningless. Do *all* things *really* work together for *good*? When millions of people—many of them Christians—die of starvation in Africa? When a church bus goes off the road and fifty kids and the driver are killed? When you get an incurable disease and are told you won't live past twenty? When your parents get divorced?

All of a sudden it seems plain that all *things* do not work together for good, even when you love God. It's easy to misunderstand the King James Version of Romans 8:28 and think that it's some kind of grisly joke.

That's why some of the newer translations say it in a different and clearer way. The New International Version says, "And we know that in all things *God works for the good of those who love him*, who have been called according to His purpose." This translation puts God in His proper place—*working in the midst of the bad things*, working to make it all come out according to

His plan and purpose, which can often be beyond our ability to see or understand.

No matter how bad "things" might be, no matter how lonely you might feel, God has a plan for you and a purpose for your life. No matter what happens to us, He is eager to accomplish His purpose for our lives.

I quoted several letters earlier that all sounded pretty lonely and desolate, but some of them have a happy ending because their writers knew where to go for help.

Michelle's letter went on to tell how she got over her hatred for the world after Sheila's tragic death:

> God was good to me through it and gave me a softer heart. At her funeral, there were four hundred thirty-seven people, all people she touched in the name of Jesus . . . Because I have hope and assurance in Jesus I know I can handle the future. As for Sheila, I know she has gone home to be with the Lord, singing praises to God face-to-face.

Terri, who suffered through rape, severe depression, and feelings of suicide, goes on to say in her letter:

> At school, it is so easy just to go through the motions. But when I remember that Jesus is the reason we are here, then I know I must do so much more than just go through the motions. Right now, I am getting over a broken relationship with my boyfriend, but God heals all things.

Heavy Questions, Exciting Answers

As Paul continues putting down his thoughts in Romans 8, he really gets wound up. He asks and answers five questions that make up one of the most incredible sections in the entire Bible. If you get ahold of what Paul is talking about in Romans 8:31–39, you'll never be the same again!

The first question asks, "What can we ever say to such wonderful things as these? If God is on our side, who can ever be against us?" (Rom. 8:31, TLB).

What if all Paul had said was, "Who is against us?" Then we could think of all kinds of enemies who could easily overwhelm us. For openers, there is Satan, the archenemy. Then there is the pressure from the crowd to do empty things to try to fill our lives. There are temptations, disease, the threat of nuclear war, accidents, racism—the list is almost endless. When Paul says, "God is on our side," we know that none of these enemies will win in the end. When it's all over, only God will be standing, and we will be standing with Him.

Paul's second question is: "Since he [God] did not spare even his own Son for us but gave him up for us all, won't he also surely give us everything else?" (Rom. 8:32, TLB).

If Paul had simply said, "Won't God surely give us everything we want?" we might have a few doubts. God does not give us everything we *want*, but He always gives us everything we *need*. And what do we need the most? We need salvation through Christ, which God gave us by not sparing His Son but giving Him up for us all.

If God could give up His Son, He isn't going to hold anything else back. As the New English Bible puts it, "How can He fail to lavish upon us all He has to give?"

Paul's third and fourth questions go together. He asks: "Who will bring any charge against those whom God has chosen? It is God who justifies. Who is he that condemns? Christ Jesus, who died—more than that, who was raised to life—is at the right hand of God and is also interceding for us" (Rom. 8:33–34, NIV).

A lot of accusers are out there ready to charge Christians with all kinds of things, from hypocrisy to being "unscientific" for not believing in evolution. Behind all these charges is Satan, who always loves to accuse Christians. In fact, the devil's very name means "slander." But the devil's accusations don't hold water because God has arranged a pardon for us. That's what justification means—being pardoned for your crimes forever.

John promises in 1 John 2:1, "If anybody does sin, we have one who speaks to the Father in our defense—Jesus Christ, the Righteous One" (NIV). Christ is the One who sticks by us and stands up for us.

John tells us in 1 John 3:20–21 that our hearts sometimes condemn us. That means that we can sometimes start thinking that we have done wrong, that we have blown it, and God surely can't put up with us any longer. I still have those thoughts at times, but no matter how badly I foul up, God knows my heart better than I do! And, if I really do get off the track, God gently helps me get back on the right track. That's what happened back when I played double agent and prodigal. Sin made my heart miserable then, and it still does. And that's when I'm thankful for God's promise to forgive when I confess (see 1 John 1:19).

It's a good idea to keep short accounts with God; don't let sin (or even what you think might be sin) pile up. Be quick to tell Him you're sorry. He will always sort it all out. Trust Him and remember: "There is now no condemnation awaiting those who belong to Christ Jesus" (Rom. 8:1, TLB).

The Greatest Question

Paul's fifth and final question is the greatest of all: "Who shall separate us from the love of Christ?" (Rom. 8:35, NIV). Paul lists every terrible thing he can think of—trouble, hardships, and persecutions, having to go hungry or even without clothes or shelter, being martyred or slaughtered. No matter what happens, "we are more than conquerors through him who loved us" (Rom. 8:37, NIV).

We are *never* alone. Christ is always with us in death or in life. Now and in the future. Whether we walk with angels or are attacked by demons. The power of hell itself cannot keep God's love away. Nothing "will be able to separate us from the love of God that is in Christ Jesus our Lord" (Rom. 8:39, NIV).[2]

You can see Romans 8:28–39 in that final chorus of "I Know":

> Now it seems that everyone's against you . . . and no one really cares . . . You don't know who to trust . . . You don't know where to turn . . . Well, at least you know you've got a prayer . . . so reach out for the One who understands you . . . Oh, He's been there . . . He knows—He knows how you feel . . . I know that He knows . . .

Here's how you can use Romans 8:28–39 on a practical daily basis. Whenever you feel yourself being squeezed hard by the world, no matter how hard things get, Scripture has an answer: **"Why does it always have to happen to me?"** In all things, God works for my good (see Rom. 8:28–30). I should not ask why something happens, but what God's purpose is for me in *this*.

"Everyone's against me." If God is for me, I cannot lose! (see Rom. 8:31). I might be alone, but I never have to be lonely because God is always there.

"I always come out on the short end of the stick." God gives me everything I need, beginning with His Son and going on from there (see Rom. 8:32).

"I've messed it up again. I'm a crummy Christian. I'm no good." Who can accuse me or condemn me? (see Rom. 8:33–34). God doesn't—in fact, Christ is my lawyer and He's never lost a case!

"If I don't go along, I won't have any friends, and I won't be able to stand it." Who can separate me from the love of Christ? (see Rom. 8:35). I can live without friends, but I can't live without Him!

Your Friend Christ

I've always had plenty of friends—of all varieties. Some of them got me into trouble, but many of them have helped pull me through and have built me up in my faith.

We've talked about friends a lot in this book, because I know how important friends can be, especially if you don't seem to have any. But if there's one thing I know, it's that Christ is my Friend, and He is yours, too. Once you settle that, you can find the other friends that you need. I know you can.

To sell out to The System, to run to "Rocketown," or to run away to Lamu to find "friends" is no answer. Jesus Christ is the ultimate Friend. He is the Light that holds you in the darkness—the Candle burning in the wind. Through Him you lean upon the Father and find the strength you need for this life.

He knows how you feel. I know that He knows. And I know that friends are friends forever when the Lord's the Lord of them!

NOTES

Chapter 1

1. Maurice Wagner, *The Sensation of Being Somebody* (Grand Rapids: Zondervan Publishing House, 1975), p. 32ff.

Chapter 4

1. Francis A. Schaeffer, *Escape from Reason* (Downers Grove, IL: InterVarsity Press, 1968), chap. 3; Schaeffer, *The God Who Is There* (Downers Grove, IL: InterVarsity Press, 1968), pp. 20–21.

Chapter 5

1. Ken Abraham, *Designer Jeans* (Old Tappan, NJ: Fleming H. Revell Company, 1986), pp. 139–41.

Chapter 7

1. Ken Abraham, *Hot Trax* (Old Tappan, NJ: Fleming H. Revell Company, 1986), p. 61. This remark is originally credited to comedian Buck Henry, who was quoted by actress Teri Garr.

Chapter 8

1. Joe White, *Friendship Pressure* (Branson, MO: Operation Challenge, n.d.), p. 12.
2. Ibid., pp. 12–13.
3. Abraham, *Hot Trax*, p. 69.

Chapter 9

1. Josh McDowell and Paul Lewis, *Givers, Takers, and Other Kinds of Lovers* (Wheaton, IL: Tyndale House Publishers, Inc., 1980), p. 33.
2. Dr. Kevin Leman, *Smart Kids, Stupid Choices* (Ventura, CA: Regal Books, 1987). (Formerly published under the title *Smart Girls Don't (and Guys Don't Either)*.)
3. Dr. Kevin Leman, *The Pleasers* (Old Tappan, NJ: Fleming H. Revell Company, 1987), chap. 7.
4. Ibid.

Chapter 10

1. Abraham, *Hot Trax*, pp. 86–87. (Adapted)

Chapter 11

1. Dan Peters and Steve Peters *Why Knock Rock?* (Minneapolis: Bethany House Publishers, 1984), pp. 160–62.
2. "The Copycat Suicides," *Newsweek*, March 23, 1987, p. 28.
3. Diane Eble, "Too Young to Die," *Christianity Today*, March 20, 1987, p. 21.

Chapter 12

1. Paul Lee Tan, *Encyclopedia of 7700 Illustrations* (Rockville, MD: Assurance Publishers, 1979), p. 753.
2. John Stott, *Men Made New* (Downers Grove, IL: InterVarsity Press, 1966), pp. 100–106. (Concept used.)

Hottest Hotlines

T he following 24-hour, toll-free numbers and Web sites are included as a service and were valid at the time of the printing of this book. However, there is no affiliation whatsoever between any of these organizations and Tommy Nelson Publishing, nor can it be held responsible for any advice given.

Abuse Counseling and Treatment, Inc. 941-939-3112 (not toll-free)

This hotline was established to give teens and adults a place to turn for completely confidential conversations, because sometimes just talking about things can help. Numerous referrals are available through the hotline.

Al-Anon or Alateen 1-800-425-2666; www.Al-anon-alateen.org

This organization provides worldwide self-help recovery for teens with friends or family members dealing with alcohol addictions. Al-Anon is not a religious organization, nor is it a professional counseling organization. It is a voluntary program with emphasis on self-help in an atmosphere of anonymity. The hotline will refer the caller to local meetings.

American Cancer Society 1-800-ACS-2345; www.ACS.org

The ACS provides information such as prevention and risk factors, detection and symptoms, treatment options, and survivorship of cancer. The Web site includes the Cancer in Children Resource Center, which deals with topics like coping with diagnosis (of cancer in children or their family members) and understanding treatment and financial issues.

ANRED (Anorexia Nervosa and Related Eating Disorders, Inc.) www.anred.com

ANRED is an information Web site that provides definitions of disorders such as anorexia, bulimia, binge eating, and compulsive exercising, as well as statistics, warning signs, medical complications, and psychological problems.

Barr-Harris Children's Grief Center 313-922-7474
(not toll-free) www.barrharris.org

The Center is designed to provide help for youth facing the pain of death, divorce, separation, or abandonment. It provides diagnostic evaluations, short- and long-term treatment, guidance, and educational programs. It is affiliated with the Institute for Psychoanalysis in Chicago.

Bethany Christian Services
1-800-Bethany; www.Bethany.org

BCS is a crisis pregnancy ministry that always encourages women to choose life. The Web site provides information on such topics as families who are waiting to adopt, birth father's rights and responsibilities, and straight talk about abortion. The hotline provides immediate confidential counseling.

Birthright International 1-800-550-4900; www.birthright.org

This organization exists to provide caring, nonjudgmental support to girls and women in crisis pregnancies. Services include friendship and emotional support; free pregnancy tests; legal, medical, and financial assistance; assistance with housing; referral to social agencies; and provision of maternity and baby clothes. Services are free and confidential.

Boys Town National Hotline 1-800-448-3000 (English or Spanish)
www.boystown.org

This organization provides care for boys and girls and for families in crisis. It has a long history of offering help, hope, and healing to abused, abandoned, neglected, handicapped, or otherwise troubled children. The hotline offers short-term intervention for any issue, including relationships, drug/alcohol abuse, or suicide.

Care-Net 1-800-395-HELP; www.care-net.org

Care-Net is an effort to provide access to the most accessible and effective abortion alternatives. Services include free pregnancy tests; birth, abstinence, and post-abortion counseling; housing; parenting classes; and help with financial, medical, and material needs.

Centers for Disease Control Prevention Resources
www.cdcnpin.org

This site provides access to hundreds of prevention resources, including the NPIN database, as well as information and referrals about HIV/AIDS.

Childhelp National Child Abuse Hotline 1-800-4-A-CHILD; www.childhelpusa.org

This privately funded, nonprofit, nonsectarian organization is dedicated to meeting the physical, emotional, educational, and spiritual needs of abused and neglected children. It provides general information about child abuse to children, adolescents, parents, and professionals, and offers professional crisis counseling. The caller can report abuse, and will be referred to local support groups and community resources for continued help.

Childnet (www.child.net/violence)

This site of violence prevention resources is one of several new, comprehensive children and youth resource guides from the Streetcats Foundation and the National Children's Coalition. Information is available about what fosters violence and what can be done to prevent it. Many links are provided to sites such as juvenile justice resources and information about gang violence.

Christians in Recovery (www.christians-in-recovery.com)

This site contains over five hundred pages of information and resources, much of it Christian. It also provides a Members Only area that includes private chat rooms, daily scheduled recovery meetings, twelve-step Bible studies, and message boards for persons dealing with recovery from addictions.

Covenant House Hotline 1-800-999-9999; www.covenanthouse.org

The Nine Line and Web site provide help for runaway youth and families through a trained staff of volunteers who offer support, assistance, and referrals to over twenty-six thousand agencies nationwide.

Crisis Hotline 713-529-TEEN or 713-HOTLINE (not toll-free) www.crisishotline.org

Crisis Intervention of Houston, Inc., is a United Way Agency dedicated to helping people in crisis through telephone crisis counseling, referrals, intervention, post-intervention, and education. Crisis workers are trained volunteers who place high emphasis on integrity, empathy, respect, and a nonjudgmental approach to the caller.

Drughelp 1-800-378-4435; www.drughelp.org

This private, nonprofit organization is a referral network providing information on specific drugs and treatment options, as well as referrals to public and private treatment programs, self-help groups, and family support groups. Immediate crisis intervention services are available over the phone.

Eating Disorders Center 1-800-541-FREE

This nonprofit agency is part of Norfolk General Hospital, and deals with anorexia, bulimia, compulsive overeating, and related problems such as depression. They offer telephone counseling and referrals to local area counselors and support groups. If volunteers are not available, the caller will be connected with Crisis Line.

Gladney Center for Adoption 1-800-433-2922; www.gladney.org

Founded more than one hundred years ago, today Gladney stands as an international leader in adoption service, specializing in international and domestic adoptions. This nonprofit center provides flexible programs for birth parents, adoptive partners, and adopted persons. The center has placed more than twenty-five thousand children in forever homes.

GriefNet www.griefnet.org

This Internet community includes thirty-five e-mail support groups and two Web sites. They are designed to approach people working through loss and grief issues of all kinds. The site includes KIDSAID, a place for kids to find information and ask questions. GriefNet is supervised by a clinical grief psychologist and is supported by a team of volunteers. It is a nonprofit corporation under the name of Rivendell Resources.

Habilitat, Inc. 1-800-235-3691; www.habilitat.org

This nonprofit organization is funded through private donations and functions as a referral and information hotline. The caller is guided toward local help, but in a crisis he/she can talk to someone who has personal experience with an addiction problem. Habilitat operates a "therapeutic community" in Keneohe Bay, Hawaii, where residents overcome problems with substance abuse, self-destructive lifestyles, and other antisocial behavior. Its success rate is three times the national average.

Harbor House (www.harborhouse.org)

This organization provides living quarters for single preteen parents (ages thirteen to nineteen) in a disciplined but loving Christian family atmosphere. It offers continued high school education, nondoctrinal teen Bible studies, and training in independent living skills.

Heartline 1-800-845-4266; www.nashvillecares.com

This Nashville-based organization provides crisis counseling, emotional support, and client referrals to those living with AIDS/HIV. There is no charge for any service.

HIV/AIDS Links from UMC (www/gbgm-umc.org/programs/hiv/aidslinks)

Sponsored by the Health and Welfare Ministries of the United Methodist Church, this computerized ministries page provides hundreds of links to HIV/AIDS ministries and networks all over the country.

Hopeline 1-800-394-HOPE; www.dawsonmcallister.com (Mon.-Thurs.: 2:00-9:00 P.M. CST; Fri.: 4:00 P.M.-Midnight; Sat.-Sun.: 7:00 P.M.-Midnight)

As part of the Dawson McAllister Association, the purpose of the Hopeline is to provide free nationwide telephone support, guidance, and direction to young people facing critical life challenges.

The Hopeline serves youth up to age twenty-one, using Scripture and biblical truths as a guidepost for problem solving. When the problems confronting these youth are too severe to be appropriately handled by phone, a referral to professional counseling or protective resources will be made.

JoinTogether www.jointogether.org

A project of the Boston University School of Public Health, JoinTogether is a national resource for communities working to reduce substance abuse and gun violence. News, information, resources and links can all be accessed from the Web site.

Missing and Exploited Children 1-800-843-5678 (English or Spanish) 1-800-826-7653 (TDY for the hearing impaired www.missingkids.com)

Callers can report missing children or report findings of missing children. Children can call and let parents know where they are.

This number is also for reporting child pornography and prostitution, including Internet pornography. Information is immediately given to U.S. Customs.

National Clearinghouse for Alcohol and Drug Information (NCADI) (www.health.org)

One of the largest federal clearinghouses, and the world's largest resource for information and materials on substance abuse. An informational service staff provides information, free and low-cost materials, and referrals to prevention, intervention, and treatment resources.

National Council on Alcoholism and Drug Dependence, Inc. (NCADD) 1-800-NCA-CALL

This affiliate referral provides education, information, help, and hope in the fight against the chronic, often fatal disease of alcoholism and other drug addictions. The Web site provides many resources and links aimed specifically at youth.

National Depression and Manic Depression Association 1-800-826-3632

This is an automated hotline where callers can request information packets about depression and manic depression.

National Drug Hotline 1-800-662-HELP

The hotline provides an automated referral-routing service for local treatment. Callers can also request printed information.

National HIV/AIDS Teen Hotline 1-800-440-8336

After hours, callers will be transferred to the Centers for Disease Control National Aids hotline for information and referral services. The CDC hotline can be reached directly at 1-800-341-AIDS or in Spanish at 1-800-344-7432.

National Runaway Switchboard 1-800-621-4000 or 1-800-621-0394 (TDD for the hearing impaired) and National Runaway Hotline 1-800-231-6946; www.nrscrisisline.org

A not-for-profit volunteer organization whose mission is to provide confidential crisis intervention and referrals to youth and their families. The Switchboard is the federally designated national communication system for runaways and homeless youth.

Information is kept completely confidential. The counselor does not need to know where the caller is unless help is needed. The agency will relay messages to the parents, and parents may return messages to their child through this group. The caller is also referred to Home Free, a service of Greyhound Bus Company.

Operation: Home Free—call local Greyhound Buslines, Inc.

Greyhound offers a free ride home to any runaway who is in custody of juvenile authorities—whether he/she was picked up or turned himself in. The police will escort the child to the bus station, and Greyhound will take him/her home.

Pregnancy Center www.pregnancycenter.org

Pregnancy Centers Online offers free Web hosting to pregnancy centers that want a Web site. These sites focus primarily on providing counseling, specifically in the form of post-abortion testimonies from counselors and women who now advocate choosing life.

RAINN (Rape, Abuse, and Incest National Network) 1-800-656-HOPE; www.rainn.org

RAINN is a nonprofit organization that is the only national hotline for survivors of sexual assault. It provides free, confidential counseling for survivors and gives information about local rape crisis centers.

The Web site includes statistics, celebrity supporter profiles, and additional contact information.

RAPHA 1-800-383-HOPE; Mon.-Fri. 8:30-6:00 P.M. EST)

RAPHA is a Christian organization that provides hospital-based as well as outpatient treatment for people in crisis situations. After business hours, calls are forwarded to counselors.

State Department of Human Services (see local directory)

This state government agency accepts reports of abused children, adults, and disabled people.

Teen Age Grief (TAG) 661-253-1932 (not toll-free) www.smartlink.net/~tag/

TAG, Inc., is a nonprofit organization with expertise in providing grief support to bereaved teens. It primarily focuses on training those who work with teens, but it does provide information and helpful links to other sites.

Teensurfer 1-800-KIDS-956; www.teensurfer.com

Created by the Streetcats Foundation and the National Children's Coalition, the site provides links to national information resources on and off the Web for problem solving and getting help for teens.

Victims of Incest Can Emerge Victorious 1-800-786-4238

After hours, this nonprofit organization will provide referrals and education through an automated helpline. Further information about surviving incest is available upon request.

Youth Crisis Hotline 1-800-448-4663; www.horizon.org

This hotline provides nondenominational support and referral services to youth who are eighteen or younger, dealing with any kind of crisis.

It's been great to have a chance to share with you some of the things that are important to me. Now I'd really like to hear back from you—about what you're struggling with and how God is helping you. Send your letter to Michael's Best Friend, P.O. Box 1341, Franklin, TN 37065, and I'll be sure to get it.

Your Friend,

Michael

Dear Michael,

_____

_____

_____

_____

_____

_____

_____

_____

Signed, _____

Acknowledgments